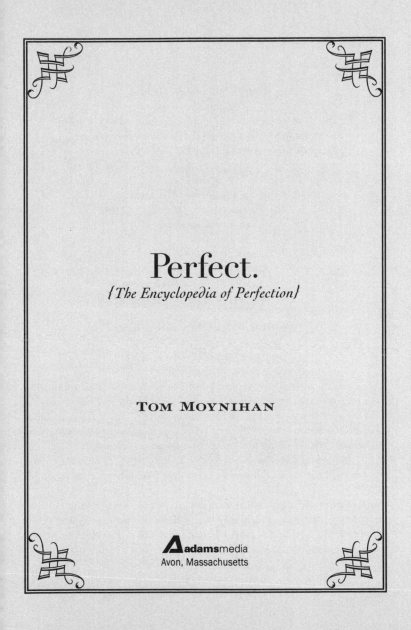

Perfect.
{The Encyclopedia of Perfection}

TOM MOYNIHAN

A adamsmedia
Avon, Massachusetts

Published by
Adams Media, a division of F+W Media, Inc.
57 Littlefield Street, Avon, MA 02322. U.S.A.
www.adamsmedia.com

ISBN 10: 1-4405-2985-X
ISBN 13: 978-1-4405-2985-6
eISBN 10: 1-4405-4019-5
eISBN 13: 978-1-4405-4019-6

Printed in the United States of America.

10   9   8   7   6   5   4   3   2   1

This publication is designed to provide accurate and authoritative information with regard to the subject matter covered. It is sold with the understanding that the publisher is not engaged in rendering legal, accounting, or other professional advice. If legal advice or other expert assistance is required, the services of a competent professional person should be sought.

—From a *Declaration of Principles* jointly adopted by a Committee of the American Bar Association and a Committee of Publishers and Associations

Many of the designations used by manufacturers and sellers to distinguish their product are claimed as trademarks. Where those designations appear in this book and Adams Media was aware of a trademark claim, the designations have been printed with initial capital letters.

This book is available at quantity discounts for bulk purchases.
For information, please call 1-800-289-0963.

Contents

Perfect . . .

Introduction

Perfect (ˈpər-fikt) *adjective*

1. being entirely without fault or defect
2. corresponding to an ideal standard or abstract concept

Source: The Merriam-Webster Dictionary

Throughout history, the human race has constantly strived for perfection. There seems to be something in our DNA that drives us to be our best, do our best, drive the best car, cook the best hamburger, write the perfect poem.

This innate quest for perfection has been part of the human experience since time immemorial. But it wasn't until some 2,500 years ago that three ancient Greeks—Socrates, Plato, and Aristotle—really developed a solid articulation of the "ideal." According to these philosophers, everything we see in the physical world—from sandwiches to sandcastles—and every concept of which we think—from competition to humor—has a perfect version, an ideal, and this ideal is what the object or thought is attempting to approximate. As a group, the human race truly believes that that ideal is right around the corner. None of what's in front of us may have achieved that, but we have faith that, with each improvement we learn to make, we inch closer to finding our ideal. Each time we take a photograph, make chicken soup, or even try on a pair of jeans, we try to get a fit that's closer to the perfect representation we have in our minds.

The entries in this book bring you one step closer to perfection. The good news is that you don't really have to labor here in your search for the ideal. Tons of other people—scientists, doctors, authors, researchers, panelists, unwitting test subjects, and even the occasional robot—have been doing all the work for you. Here you'll find info on everything from perfect pitch to the perfect pour of Guinness, from the perfect baseball game to the perfect bathroom stall to use in a public restroom. And not only will you learn what makes these things perfect, you'll also learn how to achieve a little bit of that perfection for yourself. Want to play the perfect hand of poker? Give the perfect handshake? Make the perfect martini? What are you waiting for? The answers are literally at your fingertips.

So turn the page and learn about the perfect . . .

AGE TO GET MARRIED

*H*istorically, early marriages were often of necessity; with infant mortality rates much higher than today, many women needed all the available child-birthing years they could get. In the predominantly agrarian society prior to industrialization, the only labor most people could hope to afford was their own; the sooner you got to making babies, the sooner you'd have other hands milking the cows or running the household. However, by the tail end of the 1800s in the United States, with industrialization taking over and the progeny pressure abating, the average age for men and women to get married was 26 and 22, respectively. And by 2010 the average age had increased to 28 and 24, respectively. But just because something is average doesn't mean it's perfect.

So what is the best way to determine your perfect marriage age? Fortunately, Professor Anthony Dooley at the University of South Wales School of Mathematics and Statistics has devised the following "Fiancé Formula":

1. Choose the youngest age at which you imagine you'd want to get married.
2. Choose the age that you have absolutely no intention of passing without getting married.

3. Subtract your youngest age from your oldest.
4. Multiply this number by 0.368.
5. Add the resulting number to your youngest age and you've found your unique perfect time to tie the knot!

Here's an example. Assuming that the youngest you can imagine getting married is 24 and the oldest is 36: 36 − 24 = 12; 12 × .368 = 4.416; 24 + 4.416 = 28.416. Your window of opportunity should open when you're around 28 years and 4 months old.

How does this work? Well, as the basis of his equation Dooley used the mathematical theory of optimal stopping, which involves having to make a decision to stop or continue over the course of time, as variables keep changing. The goal of such a formula is to give one a guide to stop at a point that maximizes rewards and minimizes losses.

Anticipating the criticism, Dooley admitted that relying solely on an equation to answer complex emotional questions can be "dangerous," but added that if you're hoping to decide on the "best age to start getting serious, this gives you a mathematical framework."

AGE TO RETIRE

The perfect age to retire is 62. Based on a longitudinal study lead by Esteban Calvo at Boston College in 2010, people retiring at age 62 reported substantial improvements in the way they felt both emotionally and physically and displayed fewer symptoms of depression than those retiring later. These physical and emotional improvements came after retirement, so even with their increased age, people feel better than they did when they were working. What's more, these changes lasted for years after they retired. These positive improvements were experienced regardless of the status of their health or previous presence of depression, and whether or not their retirement was voluntary. For people retiring either before or after the age of 62, these improvements not only failed to materialize, but the very same measures of well-being took a precipitous dive.

Unfortunately for seniors, this research comes just as the Social Security Administration (SSA) is increasingly urging people to put off retirement longer—at least until their full benefits kick in at age 66 or 67 depending on year of birth—so they'll put more money into the system before they start taking out. But one explanation for the findings is that the best age for people to retire *is* directly related to SSA policies. Sixty-two also happens to be the age at which a person first becomes eligible to start receiving partial Social Security benefits.

You'll receive more if you can hold off on collecting, but even the Social Security website cites the information from the Boston College Center for Retirement research. It's pretty interesting considering that, even if it doesn't serve the government's interest for most people to start collecting at 62, they aren't hiding the data that says it only pays monetarily—not physically or emotionally—to work past this age.

Still, despite the SSA's pressure to delay retirement, things have improved from where they were in the late 1800s, when the only country recognizing an official retirement age was Germany, and the general trend in other countries was to just to keep working until you either died or became physically incapable of continuing. Sixty-two's sounding pretty good now, right?

ANAGRAM

A simple anagram makes a word by rearranging all the letters that compose another word. A random anagram makes a word out of a nonsense word, like the "unscramble" puzzles found in the papers near the comics. But by definition, a *perfect* anagram is when a *meaningful* word is made from another meaningful word.

Anagrams have a long history dating back to medieval times, both as a clever game and as a mystical exploration to discover hidden messages within seemingly innocuous words. Always the most prized for its wittiness was the perfect anagram, in which the new words formed had a direct relation to the original word or words. Galileo hid his discovery of the rings of Saturn within a random anagram—smaismrmilmepoetaleumibunenugttauiras, unscrambled to the Latin "Altissimum planetam tergeminum observavi," the English translation of which is: "I have observed the highest planet tri-form"—and later, surrealist André Breton took a swipe at Salvador Dali by anagramming his name to Avida Dollars, Avida being a phonetic play of the French for "hungry." Apparently Breton wanted to indicate Dali was money hungry, and that was much more creative than yelling "sellout!" whenever Dali walked by him.

In addition, the more complex the perfect anagram, the more esteemed. For centuries, intellectuals flexed their cerebral muscles by trying to one-up each other in Latin. One of the more famous Latin anagrams is "Ave Maria, gratia plena, dominus tecum" ("Maria, full of grace, the Lord is with Thee"), which anagrams to "Virgo serena, pia, munda et immaculata" ("Virgin serene, holy, pure and immaculate"). Not impressed? Well, you would have killed with that one at a party in the Baroque era.

Modern examples of perfect anagrams include turning the words "Clint Eastwood" into "old west action," "real fun" into "funeral," and "the countryside" into "no city dust here." A modern perfect anagram is also a bit of a pseudonym. Author J. K. Rowling gave the antagonist of her *Harry Potter* series the name of Tom Marvolo Riddle, a perfect anagram of "I am Lord Voldemort." Don't say she didn't warn you.

WHAT'S IN A NAME?

Sir Peter Scott (1909–1989), one of the better-known naturalists in Britain, gave an official scientific name to the Loch Ness Monster: *Nessiteras rhombopteryx*. The name in ancient Greek means "the Ness monster with diamond-shaped fin." A reporter from the *Daily Telegraph* found that it could make the anagram "Monster Hoax by Sir Peter S." Undeterred, Sir Peter Scott went on to cofound the Loch Ness Phenomena Investigation Bureau in 1962.

Perfect . . .

ART HEIST

*O*ver the years there have been a whole lot of art heists, like 2008's E. G. Bürle Foundation heist in Switzerland, the 1991 theft of twenty paintings at Amsterdam's Van Gogh Museum, and the multiple thefts of Munch's *The Scream* in 2004 and 2006 (a different version of this painting was also stolen in 1994). But the robbery at the Isabella Stewart Gardner Museum in Boston on March 18, 1990, was really the perfect crime. So perfect, in fact, that the FBI's lead agent on the case, Geoffrey Kelly, called it "the heist of the century."

On Sunday, March 18, 1990 at 1:24 A.M., two police officers approached the side door of the Isabella Stewart Gardner Museum, which served as the security entrance, and one of them knocked. Twelve years later the Museum's head of security, Lyle Grindle, told a security trade publication that "policy has always been that you don't open that door in the middle of the night for God."

But at that early hour of March 18, told by the officers that they were there responding to a call, the security guard did just that. Inside, the officers asked the guard to come out from behind the security desk, and he complied. The officers then said they recognized him and that there was a warrant out for his arrest. They told him to radio the other security guard to come meet them, which he also did. When the security guard realized he wasn't being frisked, and inquired about it, the "officers" admitted they were there to commit a robbery, and told the man if he did as he was told, he wouldn't get hurt. The guard then replied, "Don't worry, they don't pay me enough to get hurt." The two robbers promptly handcuffed both guards and left them in the museum's basement locked to pipes, some forty feet from each other, with their heads, hands, and feet bound with duct tape.

In just under an hour and a half, the two nonpolicemen toured the museum and made off with *The Concert*, one of the thirty-four works known by Vermeer; *Chez Tortoni* by Manet; a finial from a Napoleonic flag in the shape of an eagle; five drawings by Degas; and three works by Rembrandt. The thieves have never been found, and neither has any of the artwork, which has an estimated total value of $500 million.

One of the more baffling aspects of the robbery is why some pieces were stolen and other pieces of great value were simply passed over. But even as that debate raged, those in both the art and law enforcement worlds were pondering the practicality of stealing "too hot" items that the likes of only a Bond villain would purchase.

The perfection of the heist lies not in its precision, but in its utter success and the air of mystery surrounding it over the course of more than two decades. And as time passes, statute-of-limitation issues come into play, making it harder for the thieves to be prosecuted. That is, if anyone could ever find them . . .

Perfect . . .

BASEBALL GAME

When a pitcher, for a minimum of nine innings, keeps each and every opposing batter from reaching first base, it's said he pitched a "perfect game." To date, there have been only twenty-one perfect games in baseball's entire history. Though the term is often applied to the pitcher, a perfect game isn't necessarily all his doing. The team only needs to prevent anyone from the opposing team reaching base, and this can happen if a batter strikes out, gets a hit that's then caught in the air, or gets a hit but is thrown out before reaching first base.

PLAYERS WHO HAVE PITCHED PERFECT GAMES
- Lee Richmond—June 12, 1880
- John Montgomery Ward—June 17, 1880
- Cy Young—May 5, 1904
- Addie Joss—October 2, 1908
- Charlie Robertson—April 30, 1922
- Don Larsen—October 8, 1956
  (only perfect game in the postseason to date)
- Jim Bunning—June 21, 1964
- Sandy Koufax—September 9, 1965
- Catfish Hunter—May 8, 1968

- Len Barker—May 15, 1981
- Mike Witt—September 30, 1984
- Tom Browning—September 16, 1988
- Dennis Martinez—July 28, 1991
- Kenny Rogers—July 28, 1994
- David Wells—May 17, 1998
- David Cone—July 18, 1999
- Randy Johnson—May 18, 2004
- Mark Buehrle—July 23, 2009
- Dallas Braden—May 9, 2010
- Roy Halladay—May 29, 2010
- Philip Humber—April 21, 2012

A no-hitter is a game in which one team (or both) fails to get a hit throughout the entire game, which has to last at least nine innings. A no-hitter is generally earned by one pitcher who pitches the whole game, but it can also be done by multiple pitchers within the same game. Also, it's possible that even though a team is pitching a no-hitter, the opposing team can not only get on base but also score without hitting a single ball, simply by the pitcher walking a batter. From 1875 to 2011, only 272 games have been recorded as no-hitters, and of those, twenty-five were games in which the team without a hit scored.

There are years when no one throws a no-hitter, and sometimes those are consecutive. As of 2011, the largest number of consecutive years to go by without a no-hitter is three. Nolan Ryan holds the record as the pitcher with the most no-hitters, having thrown seven during his career. As far as pitchers go, one of the more notable no-hitters was thrown by Jim Abbott who, having been born without a right hand, pitched a no-hitter against the Cleveland Indians in 1993 when he was with the Milwaukee Brewers.

THE IMPERFECT GAME

On June 2, 2010, Armando Galarraga was pitching for the Detroit Tigers as they played the Cleveland Indians. The first twenty-six batters to come to the plate left without a base among them, and he seemed to be headed for a perfect game. But with two outs in the ninth inning, Jason Donald of the Indians hit a grounder. Galarraga covered first and, as clearly as all could see, Donald was out. Galarraga would have his perfect game and would be only the twenty-first pitcher to do so—except for the fact that first-base umpire Jim Joyce seemed to suffer from a hallucination at the same time and called Donald safe. Instant replay isn't allowed in baseball, and the call stood. After the game Joyce apologized, tearfully, to Galarraga in front of the media for his bad call. The game is often referred to as the "Galarraga game," the "28-out perfect game," or the "Imperfect Game." For his part, Galarraga took the whole incident with an air of calm acceptance, bearing no ill will, simply saying to reporters after the game, "Nobody's perfect."

Perfect . . .

BATHROOM STALL TO CHOOSE WHEN FACED WITH MORE THAN TWO

According to University of Arizona microbiologist Charles Gerba, the cleanest stall is the first one. According to research done by Dr. Gerba, aka Dr. Germ, it's the middle stall in most public bathrooms that has proven to be the "germiest."

A 1995 study, "Choices From Identical Options," by Nicholas Christenfeld with the University of California–San Diego, published in *Pyschological Science* (Volume 6, January, 1995), concurs with Gerba. Christenfeld's study found that people, when presented with options bearing no discernable differences, are predisposed to go for the "thing" in the middle. This was found to be true in grocery stores, which often stock a particular item that sells well in multiple rows of identical and accessible product, but end up having to restock those in the middle significantly more often. The study found the same to be true when it came to bathroom stalls, where usage was determined by monitoring the number of toilet paper rolls in each stall that had to replaced over time. But this preference for the middle doesn't end with the stalls. When there are more than two toilet paper dispensers in a row, the roll that needs replacing the most is the middle one.

The cleanliness of the first stall can also be attributed to its location near the door. According to the John Tesh radio show in 2007, the first stall's proximity to the door and thus the outside world "doesn't feel private enough." Allison Janse, author of *The Germ Freak's Guide to Outwitting Colds and Flu,* agrees with the first-stall theory, and adds in her book, "If you have the option, choose a bathroom with more than one stall, since more bacteria build up on a single stall." Less bathroom bacteria? Sounds pretty perfect!

However, if you do use a restroom with only one stall or if you're forced to use the stall in the middle, it may help to bear in mind that the contents of chamber pots were once dumped unceremoniously into the gutters and ran along the side of the streets. Suddenly even portable potties seem cleaner.

Bathroom Banter

While many people are mindful or even phobic of the germ factor of the bathroom, a 2010 study by Georgia-Pacific reported that a whopping 86 percent of people surveyed put aside the "eww" factor to have personal conversations in the bathroom. The top subject? Their work, giving a literal twist to the expression "dirty jobs."

BODY TEMPERATURE

*Y*ou don't feel well and are worried that you may have a fever. You take your temperature and, once you see 98.6°F, you relax in the knowledge that all is well. But why 98.6°F? Why not 94.3°F? Or 102.9°F? Or maybe something more comfortable, say, around room temperature?

According to a group of researchers at the Albert College of Medicine, with each increase in body temperature of 1.8°F, you make yourself an inhospitable habitat for an additional 6 percent of fungus varieties. However, if your body temperature was too much higher than 98.6°F, your body would require much more food to maintain itself. So the human body settled on a temperature that's not so hot that you have to eat incessantly to provide the energy necessary to maintain the temperature, but still hot enough that only a few hundred fungal species find you easy pickings. That may sound like a lot, but it's relative to the tens of thousands of species that can't take the heat and instead bother the much cooler reptiles and amphibians. Researchers conclude that our arrival at this body temperature can be fully explained by the need to arrive at an efficient balance, and note that our "normal" temperature came about during a period of fungal bloom that occurred at the end of the Cretaceous Period, setting the stage for a mammalian and eventually human advantage in relation to other vertebrates during the Tertiary Period.

Though 98.6°F degrees is the perfect norm, this temperature will vary to some degree by the individual, and whether the person is hungry, cold, or recently awakened. Your temperature will also be different depending on whether it's measured orally or internally. For the common at-home method, under the tongue, the general range is 97.7°F to 99.5°F.

High Maintenance

The human body has a remarkable number of mechanisms to maintain its temp at 98.6°F, including sweating and expanding or constricting the blood vessels in the skin. In extreme cold, those priorities shift and the blood goes to protect your vital organs, leaving your skin feeling cold. As cold exposure continues, a person will actually perceive *less* cold as hypothermia sets in, and by the time the body temp is at the possibly lethal 88°F, the person will have stopped shivering.

Perfect . . .

BOWLING GAME

he most popular version of bowling is tenpin, in which a perfect game is reached by twelve consecutive strikes—one in each of the first nine frames and then three in the tenth—for a total score of 300. In the early days of bowling, perfect games were difficult to accomplish and generally a rarity, but as technological advancements in lanes, shoes, pins, and balls took off in the 1970s, perfect games became more frequent. In the 1968–1969 bowling season the American Bowling Congress (now the United States Bowling Congress, or USBC) recorded 905 perfect games. By the 1998–1999 season, that number ballooned to 34,470. In reality, the number of perfect games actually bowled is most likely higher than what's recorded, since a major bowling association must inspect and approve of the lane conditions on which the game was played in order for it to be officially recognized as perfect.

In league play there is a 900 series, an accomplishment consisting of three 300-point games. As with individual games, official recognition of reaching a perfect series has to be approved, and that doesn't always come easy. In 1997 the first officially recorded 900 series was achieved by college bowler Jeremy Sonnenfeld. Prior to the official recording, beginning in 1982 (when the first reported perfect series was achieved by Glenn Allison), there were six previous 900 series, all disqualified (including Allison's) for technical infractions, some of which are still debated. The increase in frequency of perfect series over the years is evident in the statistics: From 1982 through 1997, there were only six reported perfect series, and each was disqualified. The USBC then listed twelve perfect series between 1997 and 2008, and six in 2009 and 2010 alone.

A More Difficult Perfect

Bowler Dale Davis judged his rolls on three things: how each felt leaving his fingers, the sounds it made hitting the pins, and someone telling him he'd thrown a strike. A World War II veteran, the seventy-eight-year-old Davis had complete loss of sight due to macular degeneration when he scored a perfect game in 2008—the first for someone with complete forward vision loss.

Perfect . . .

BOXING RECORD

*P*erfection in sports—especially boxing—isn't always pretty. Boxing historian Nate Fleischer maintains that boxer Rocky Marciano was "crude, wild swinging, awkward and missed heavily." Still, to date, Marciano is the only heavyweight champion to retire with a perfect record.

The son of Italian immigrants, Marciano was born in 1923 and, like every great underdog, started out in life against the odds, almost dying from pneumonia when was eighteen months old. As a kid, he punched a stuffed mailbag in the backyard, and worked out with weights that he made himself. After he was drafted by the Army in World War II, he won the 1946 Amateur Armed Forces Boxing Tournament, which got him started on his path to perfection.

After failing to make the cut for a farm team of the Chicago Cubs, Marciano returned to boxing. His first professional fight was in 1948, and he started his career with a knockout, an end result that repeated itself over and over again for his next fifteen fights. In nine of these fights, Marciano won by knockout before the bell in the first round, and the rest all occurred before the fifth round. In late December of 1949 he stepped into the ring with Carmine Vingo, and knocked him out in the sixth round with such force that Vingo suffered a brain hemorrhage in the ring and spent the next three days in a coma.

In 1952, when he was twenty-eight, Marciano became the Heavyweight Champion of the World, and won his last fight defending the title in 1955 in the ninth round by knockout. He retired in 1956, having won each of his forty-nine fights, forty-three of them by knockout.

BUILDING

ritish painter William Hodges described it in 1783: "It appears like a perfect pearl on an azure ground. The effect is such I have never experienced from any work of art." American writer Bayard Taylor (1825–1878) said of this building, "So pure, so gloriously perfect did it appear that I almost feared to approach it lest the charm should be broken." Of what miracle of architecture do these artists speak? None other than the Taj Mahal.

Built by Mughal (descendants of Timurids and Genghis Khan) emperor Shah Jahan starting in 1632, with completion around 1653, the building is actually an elaborate tomb and memorial for Jahan's wife, Mumtaz Mahal, who died at age thirty-eight while giving birth to their fourteenth child; the daughter, Gauhara Begun, survived and lived to be seventy-five. After Mahal's death, it is said Jahan withdrew into mourning for a year, came out of it stooped and gray haired, and was shortly unseated from power by one of his sons.

A marvel of modern architecture, the Taj Mahal, which poet Rabindranath Tagore describes as "a teardrop on the cheek of eternity," was named a World Heritage Site in 1986 by the United Nations Educational, Scientific, and Cultural Organization (UNESCO). Thousands of artists and craftspeople worked on the building under the supervision of Ustad Ahmad Lahauri, Makramat Khan, and Abdul ul-Karim Ma'mur Khan, although it is thought Jahan himself had a significant hand in the design. Lahauri, who was probably Persian, is thought to have been the main architect.

The Taj Mahal is a series of structures, best known for its famous dome, which is 120 feet high and 70 feet in diameter. Jewels and the world's finest building materials compose this tribute to love, with the white marble reflecting the changing colors of the sky. It took a team of a thousand elephants to transport the marble from the quarry two hundred miles away. The Taj was the first building in the area to use inlaid wall art of semiprecious stones like lapis lazuli, onyx, topaz, and jasper.

The building, like other things found "perfect," is extremely symmetrical, with matching domes, towers, platforms, minarets, and even a reflecting pool. The gardens and their waterways also are symmetrical. The symmetry of the building is only imperfect in two places: in one leaning minaret, which was not a mistake but actually earthquake proofing to protect the rest of the building should the minaret fall; and the simultaneously lovely and sad placement of Shah Jahan's coffin next to that of his wife. Mumtaz Mahal's coffin had already been placed in the exact center of the mausoleum, so Jahan's coffin is a slight disruption to that symmetry. Art historian Shobita Punja describes the building well: "The Taj is the synthesis of so many religions, many architectural forms, many artistic traditions. That is why it's so perfect. It's a symbol of perfect love and great beauty."

Perfect . . .

BULL RIDE

$\mathcal{A}$ perfect bull-riding score of 100 was achieved by Wade Leslie in Central Point, Oregon, in 1991. He remains the only rider with a perfect score. Prior to that, the highest score was 98 by Denny Flynn in Palestine, Illinois, in 1979.

Beginning in the mid-1800s there were bullfights in Texas, owing to its close proximity to Mexico, where bullfighting was popular, but by the early 1890s it had been banned by the state. At about the same time, rodeos had begun, initially using castrated bulls, which were a little more controllable. All it took to get the public interested in the sport was to switch out the steers for more rambunctious intact bulls, and the sport grew. Still, it wasn't until 1994 that bull riding had its own dedicated organization, the Professional Bull Riders.

The highest score a bull rider can get on a "ride" is 100. The rider has to stay on for eight seconds to qualify and receive a score. As soon as the bull passes the plane of the gate, the clock starts running. The clock will stop when the eight seconds are up or if the rider's free arm touches the bull, the rider touches the ground, or the rider's hand comes out of the rope. There are four judges, and each scores the rider on a scale of 1 to 25. The results from the judges are added together, and then half of the score is given to the rider and the other half to the bull, so that each scores between 1 and 50. When added together again, the total score for the ride falls between 1 and 100.

LEGENDARY LANE

One of the more famous bull riders was Lane Frost. His fame came from both his occasionally acrobatic showmanship and his untimely riding-related death in 1989 at the age of twenty-five in Cheyenne, Wyoming, where Frost's ribs were broken by a bull's horn in the ring. Although no autopsy was ever performed, it is believed the broken ribs severed arteries to his heart. Lane's story was immortalized in the 1994 film *8 Seconds*.

Perfect . . .

BURGER, GRILLED

Burgers tend to be forever lumped together with hot dogs and yellow mustard, suggesting they have the sophistication of a chicken nugget. But burgers, when done right, are a true culinary experience. Steve Raichlen, author of *The Barbecue Bible* and host of the television show *Primal Grill,* stated in an interview with *Popular Mechanics* that perfect burgers are the result of following these instructions:

1. Start with a half-and-half mixture of ground chuck (for flavor) and ground sirloin (for class). The fat content should be between 10 and 15 percent. The fat is the seat of flavor, so you need to achieve a balance between enough to offer great taste, but not so much that you serve big bites of grease. You'll find that balance at 15 percent. If you're looking for something with less fat but don't want to lose flavor, try bison as a tasty alternative to hamburger.

2. The meat should be kept cold, and keeping your hands wet with cold water will help. When shaping the patties, try to handle the meat as little as possible to avoid warming it up, or "bruising" it, or overcompressing it, which will result in dry burgers. You'll often see someone make a patty, squish it back into a ball, and then remake the patty. Don't do this; it is the stuff of amateurs.

3. For firm patties that won't fall apart on the grill, make your burgers a few hours before you plan to cook them and chill them in the fridge or cooler, on a plate covered with plastic wrap. Leave them chilled until the last minute.

4. Before you grill, brush the burgers on both sides with extra virgin olive oil or melted butter. This will keep the burgers from sticking to the grill and will add flavor. There's no need to obsess about seasoning; Raichlen uses only sea salt and coarsely ground pepper.

5. Just because you're grilling doesn't mean all the usual rules of hygiene can be tossed out. Hopefully you wouldn't cook in a pan that you used two weeks ago and didn't clean, and the grill is no different. If it's not clean, clean it.

6. To give your burger the classic grill marks, after putting them on the grill wait about two minutes and then give them each a quarter turn. The perfect burger is only flipped once. When you see a couple beads of blood coming up through the top or the edges start to brown, there's your moment to flip. Follow the 30 percent rule, which is to leave that percentage of the grill open. This prevents overcrowding and gives you a place to quickly move burgers during a "flare-up." The popular habit of putting the spatula on top of cooking burgers and squeezing down, often for no reason other than we seem to think we're supposed to, accomplishes nothing except covering the fire with the burger juices. "Do not, I repeat, do not press on a burger with a spatula while it's grilling," says Raichlen.

7. When the burgers are done, let them sit off the heat for a few minutes before doling them out. This lets the meat "relax," and results in a juicier burger. It's true people like the taste of medium or rare burgers, but they also tend to be averse to food poisoning. Your burgers should register at least 160°F before

you consider them done. To compensate, you can mix a little cheese into the patties when you shape them, which will melt when cooked and will make even well-done burgers moist, or you can put a little dab of herbed butter in the center of the burger.

8. Last, grill the burgers for one to two minutes.

When you follow these steps to perfection, note that there's no evidence that grilling can be either helped or hampered by appreciative or speculative grunts or idle comments about the meat, the weather, or the beer you're drinking, so don't be shy about keeping that uber-traditional.

Perfect . . .

CAR

So you want to drive the "perfect car." One that's great for the environment, looks great in your garage, and can go from 0 to 60 mph in 1.2 seconds. You want to live the dream . . .

And a dream it is, because the perfect car has yet to be invented. That's because every car currently on the market suffers from a fatal flaw. Cars that are great for the environment aren't zippy or particularly sexy. Cars that are sexy, such as the drool-worthy Bugatti Veyron, are awful for the planet. The Veyron can produce 1,001 horsepower and has a top speed of more than 250 miles per hour, which is enough to give anyone an adrenaline rush, but, it also uses 1.33 gallons of gas *per minute*. And that's not even taking into consideration the $2 million price tag.

The good news is that you can now hear the engine of the perfect car revving right over the horizon. BMW is working furiously to achieve perfection with its "i" brand line of cars, which are gas free, environmentally friendly, safe, reliable, affordable, and of course . . . stylish. Sure, the i3 concept car is not as fast as the Veyron (it accelerates from 0 to 62 mph in eight seconds), but you won't have to sell your soul to own it and you'll feel good and hip driving it.

In the meantime, it seems the American public has accidentally voted the Ford F- Series pickup truck the perfect vehicle, as it's been the top seller in the United States for an astonishing twenty-four years. Unfortunately, this vehicle chugs gas and gets a measly fourteen miles per gallon—which is a far from desirable statistic, but unforgivable considering it goes from 0 to 60 mph in about seven seconds. Yawn. Another car that some consider perfect (it was the top consumer-rated car of 2012 according to Kelley Blue Book) is the 2012 Suzuki Kizashi. The Kizashi retails for approximately $24,000, was rated number one for performance and comfort, and came in a close third place for reliability. But, in the crucial category of fuel economy it ranked fourteenth, with 30 miles per gallon.

Many consumers hoped the growing number of hybrid options would hold the key to the perfect car, but sadly, toxic batteries power these vehicles. Toyota and Honda used a battery made of sealed nickel metal hydride, which does not contain sulfuric acid like some batteries, but the production of the battery and the electric motor is detrimental to the environment. As a matter of fact, in Toyota's 2009 North America Environmental Report and in a 2007 article in *The Recorder*, author Chris Demorro makes a case that the Prius actually causes more environmental damage than the infamous Hummer due to the danger of nickel plants and the impracticality of production.

So, what's your perfect car? It depends. The experts at Edmunds suggest you consider a variety of factors. These include the number of occupants you'll want to transport, how much storage capacity you need, the price range you're willing to spend within, what kind of technology or bells and whistles you'd like, how many miles per gallon you're looking to get, what sort of performance you want, and how much safety you need. Input those factors into the Edmunds website (*www.edmunds.com*)—or a host of others—and they'll spit out some "perfect car" options specially tailored for you and your needs, which may be pretty close to perfect after all.

Perfect . . .

CAT

While the perfect cat breed would be hotly contested among cat lovers, the breed found perfect for the widest segment of the population is the American Shorthair. The Shorthair has eighty different colors that are recognized by the Cat Fanciers' Association, with common ones being tabby, brown, black, or white. These cats have short fur and long tails. The American Shorthair is one of the most popular breeds adopted by families, but it scores high in all categories most considered for breed selection, such as the animal's predisposition to be active, playful, and ability to be independent. Other considerations include:

- The cat's affection level
- Ability to thrive with other pets and children
- The amount of work involved in grooming the animal
- Intelligence
- Friendliness
- Aggression levels

American Shorthairs receive straight A's on the report card when judged on all of these factors.

Originally brought to North America by British colonists, Shorthairs were first prized for controlling rodent populations on the long and dangerous voyage across the Atlantic. Once settled on land, people discovered that this breed's virtues extended past cheap pest control and into the realm of pleasant companionship. To this day, American Shorthairs remain excellent mousers, but also maintain a gentle demeanor.

This loyal and affectionate breed is good for both single people and families. They are good with children and even amiable to dogs. They enjoy play but usually aren't overly active or house destroyers. Another beloved aspect of this breed is its quietness. While beautiful and exotic breeds like the Siamese have their devoted followings, their meows are frequent and piercing. The American Shorthair will occasionally meow, but it will also not wake the household before dawn because a leaf blew by the window.

No breed is immune to health problems, but the American Shorthair may save on vet bills and stress with its strong constitution and long life span of fifteen to twenty years. The top health issue for this breed is obesity due to overfeeding. Its short coat requires little maintenance; weekly brushing may prevent hairballs and control shedding.

American Shorthairs are often misunderstood as a breed and are often considered to be the same as Domestic Shorthairs. While American Shorthair is a specific pedigree, Domestic Shorthair refers to a cat of mixed, unspecified, or unknown breeding. For a period of time the two names were considered the same, until the Cat Fanciers' Association reclaimed the American Shorthair distinction in 1966. In the years that followed, this breed really took off to become the "perfect" cat that many households know and love. The Cat Fanciers' Association acknowledges America's favorite breed and sums up the many positive qualities of the American Shorthair by describing it as "truly a star in the feline world."

Possibly Purrfect

The perfect cat for anyone with specific needs is a shelter cat. Adoption counselors become quickly familiar with the personalities of each animal and help make perfect matches. While kittens are often irresistible, an older cat with an established personality makes a more reliable selection. An Associated Press/Petside.com poll revealed that 84 percent of people who adopted from a shelter found it to be a positive experience. Look to adopt your own American Shorthair at *www.petfinder.com*.

Perfect . . .

COMPETITION

*I*n economic theory, "perfect competition" exists as an abstract idea, rather than a real practice. Within this theory, perfect competition describes an economic environment in which lots of people are making and selling things, and lots of people are buying them. What makes it "perfect" is the idea that supply and demand are behaving in their ideals: There are several companies making similar products, so if one becomes too expensive, people will switch to one of the other "brands," which ensures that costs stay under control, and no company or producer has any leverage.

In perfect competition there are four characteristics:

1. The industry/market consists of a large number of small companies
2. The companies all sell similar products
3. There is an ability for new companies to enter and leave the industry without much effect
4. There is a perfect knowledge of technology and prices, for both sellers and buyers

When these four characteristics are all in place, consumers have choice, which makes it impossible for any individual company to gain an inordinate amount of sway or direct the market for its own purposes. Perfect knowledge means each player is operating on the same playing field, that buyers are aware of all the substitutes/choices that are available, and that these choices do exist. With easy entry into the market, no company is able to set up barriers such as patents.

On the other end of the spectrum is a monopoly, in which there is one producer/seller for a specific product in a given market; with no competition, there is no natural counter to high prices. The one producer is not just a company any more, it is the industry itself. In a monopoly market structure, it's extremely difficult for a new company to enter a market. For example, if stores only sell one kind of computer, it's virtually impossible for another computer manufacturer to enter the picture if it doesn't have anywhere to sell its computers. Monopolies can also exist due to a patent, which can make it impossible for someone else to manufacture the same thing. A common example of this is in the pharmaceutical industry, when a particular drug is exorbitantly priced until it becomes open to generic manufacturing, as detailed in a 2005 report "The Choice: Healthcare for People or Drug Industry Profits" from the nonprofit, nonpartisan organization Families USA.

Perfect competition is generally considered to be just a theory, but there are a few examples of trade that come very close to being defined that way. One example is currency dealing, in which there is always a homogenous market. In any foreign city, a U.S. dollar is still a USD. Banks, hedge funds, corporate banks, and even tourists worldwide constitute the buyers and sellers. Thanks to technology, everyone involved is well informed, and once again, a USD is a USD. It's not a type of shampoo that a different company can put in a fancy bottle and sell at three times the price. No one is going to pay more for a USD because it has a ribbon on it, or because only one bank controls the flow of all USD's and thus can determine the price at whim.

Another example that's close to perfect competition is an open-air market, like the Grande Place in Brussels, Belgium, where vendors sell similar goods at the same prices. There are a large number of buyers, no entry or exit fees, and it's just as easy to reach one seller as any other. This small reflection of perfect competition dates back to the markets of medieval Europe (as easily imagined when in the Grande Place today), and also exists in modern times with street vendors in developing countries selling similar foods, for the same price, in the same place.

It may be just a theory, but when wandering the Grande Place with a warm, delicious waffle in hand, and picking out your variety of fresh produce or European keepsakes, it's easy to applaud the idea of perfect competition.

Six of One, Half Dozen of the Other

Perfect competition only exists where the similar products made by different companies are "perfect substitutes" for each other. If they're not of similar quality, or for some other reason not held in the same esteem by a consumer, the paradigm falls apart. In real life, both instances are widespread.

CREDIT

*I*f you want to buy a house, get a car loan, or even sometimes land a coveted job, the number you ideally want to see come up as your credit score is a big old 850, the number signifying perfect credit. The now-standard score didn't exist until the late 1980s, and is based on a scale of 300 being the lowest and 850 being "perfect" and the highest. This scale was originally created in the 1950s by engineer Bill Fair of Fair, Isaac and Company, but would take another thirty years to introduce a general purpose score and have its usage achieve popularity. Fair, Isaac and Company would later be renamed "Fair Isaac Corporation," which is how it was known until 2009, when it rebranded as "FICO."

Some people (possibly an endangered species) actually have a perfect score of 850. Unfortunately, if you don't currently have an 850, you probably never will, even if you do everything possible to achieve it, including the following:

- Pay all your bills on time
- Maintain a low debt-to-credit ratio
- Rarely open new accounts
- Pay a monthly service that allows you to methodically check and monitor your report regularly to verify that all the information is true

The reason that an 850 is often unachievable, according to FICO spokesman Craig Watts, is that there is not one single method for computing your score, but ten. Each of these methods, says Watts, acts as a "scorecard" that will run through the items in your report and weight them differently depending on where you are in your credit history and how you compare to your peers. If you are a student with virtually no credit history, your score is determined by a FICO formula comparing you to others with similarly short credit histories. There's even a different scorecard applied for people who've previously reported bankruptcy. By federal law, negative information on your report such as late payments can only stay on your report for seven years. Positive records, however, can remain indefinitely.

What this means, Watts explains, is that each scorecard has its own range of scores, and if the upper range of your particular scorecard doesn't reach 850, neither will you. Further, you won't be told which scorecard you're being judged by or when you might graduate to a different category. That said, people with scores in the 800s generally have been managing credit for twenty years or more, says Watts, and the longer you've had credit, the better your chances of being on a scorecard that has an 850 at the top. Until you reach that point, he says, pay on time and take on new credit only when absolutely necessary. While an 850 might be perfect, anything over 800 is considered an "elite" score that will open a plethora of low-interest offers and deals.

Credit is infamous for being an imperfect system, and has maintained that reputation for the approximate century it's been in practice. Overly sensitive or flatly erroneous reporting can keep the average consumer far from the elusive 850. Still, pro–credit scoring economists make the sharp point that prior to these scores, lending was based on local gossip—but in reality it also involved a face-to-face meeting to discuss a borrower's financial situation, and for the lender to assess their character.

CRIME

"*P*erfect crimes" are those so cleverly designed they can't be solved, so subtly executed that they go completely unnoticed, or crimes in which people are caught or suspected, but due to some technicality or lack of evidence cannot legally be found guilty. Outside of violent crime, the perpetrators of perfect crimes are often begrudgingly given a degree of respect for pulling off a caper that so successfully confounds detectives, forensic investigators, lawyers, and other law enforcement professionals.

The story of what was considered by widely circulated sources such as *Time* magazine and *ABC News* to be a perfect crime was that of a good ol' fashioned jewel theft. In January of 2009, an upscale seven-story German department store, Kaufhaus des Westens, was robbed of jewelry valued at $6.8 million. Three glove-wearing masked men were caught on surveillance tape. When investigators took a walk around, it appeared the robbery had been accomplished in *Mission Impossible* style. The thieves had descended from the skylights and outmaneuvered the security system with rope ladders. There were no fingerprints to be found anywhere, and detectives didn't have any leads.

Police thought they'd made a break in the case when, at the foot of a ladder the thieves had used to reach the first floor, they found a latex glove that had been left behind. On it was a single drop of sweat. But when they ran the results of the DNA test through the German crime database, they didn't get one hit—they got two.

Twenty-seven-year-old Lebanese identical twins Hassan and Abbas O—German law prohibits the release of their full names—had lived in Germany since they were a year old, but were not yet citizens. They both were arrested and both charged with burglary, and each faced a possible ten-year sentence. But the court had to let them go. Identical twins share 99.99 percent of their DNA, and the minute differences between them can only be found in spontaneous mutations residing in various organs and tissues. The court was informed that they would literally have to dissect the brothers to assign guilt. Thus the German authorities were forced to release both brothers. "From the evidence we have, we can deduce that at least one of the brothers took part in the crime, but it has not been possible to determine which one," the official court statement read.

The brothers need to watch their behavior, because if new evidence emerges, they could face prosecution. However, due to their current status, their phones cannot be tapped, nor can their bank accounts be monitored. Conveniently for them, they are also both free to travel, but flashing any bling while doing so would be ill-advised.

TRIAL OF THE CENTURY

In 1924, Nathan Freudenthal Leopold Jr. and Richard Albert Loeb murdered Loeb's neighbor and second cousin, fourteen-year-old Robert "Bobby" Franks. The loose end that nailed them was a pair of glasses found near Robert's body; Leopold owned one of the three pairs sold in Chicago. They may not have committed the perfect crime, but their trial became such a media circus it was one of the first to be tagged the "Trial of the Century."

Perfect . . .

CUP OF COFFEE

*T*here is a science and art to brewing the perfect cup of coffee—despite what the proliferation of burnt coffee grounds and cold cups of coffee-flavored water may make you think—and food scientist Chris Young has the right credentials to create that perfect cuppa joe. His technique was developed with help from World Barista Champions (yes, that's a thing) James Hoffman and Tim Wendlebow. To create the best cup, try the following:

- Grind the beans with a burr grinder, which is uncommon for home use, but the only way to get a uniform particle distribution. Use a coarse grind. Freshly ground beans make a significant improvement to flavor because grinding the beans releases gasses, which may be trapped in a vacuum pack but will be lost quickly after it's been opened, as breaking the vacuum exposes the beans to oxygen, which begins a chemical reaction that degrades the coffee beans and makes them stale.

- Experiment to find your perfect brewing time. For Young, it's four minutes. He suggests not covering while steeping, to let the grounds "bloom." Hoffman suggests brewing at 175°F for "simplistic sweetness," and reminds, "the more heat you have, the more extraction you have."

Hoffman and Wendlebow suggest using a French press, with a ratio of 70 grams of coffee per liter of water. A French press is a way of brewing coffee by infusion, just like a countertop drip brewing machine, with hot water flowing over the grounds. The other popular form of brewing is percolation, where water flows through the coffee, bringing with it the soluble molecules. Percolation will likely bring up a debate among coffee aficionados, as some dismiss it as creating a bitter brew. Many others hold the typical 1950s style gurgling percolator in a dreamy nostalgic reverie, and will argue the coffee it produces is hotter and more flavorful. Whatever method you choose, remember that coffee is 98 percent water, so use quality spring or filtered water. Distilled water lacks the minerals that complement the flavor of the coffee.

Of course, the beans themselves are critical when you're striving for perfection. According to CoffeeReview.com, the top-rated beans of 2011–2012 are:

- Kenya AA Wamamuga from Paradise Roasters
- Panama Esmeralda Special from P.T.'s Roasting Company
- Kenya Mamuto from Terrior Coffee
- Esmeralda Especial Best of Panama from The Roasterie
- Ethiopia Washed Yirgacheffe, Koke Grade 1 from Simon Hsieh's Aroma Roast Coffees
- Guatemalan Hunapu Antigua Bourbon from Temple Coffee and Tea
- Kenyan Nyeri AB Gichatha-ini Signature Series from Wood-Fire Roasted Coffee
- "Kona Sweet" 100 percent Kona from Hula Daddy

One of the world's most expensive coffees, made famous by the film *The Bucket List*, is Kopi Luwak, which is produced when an animal called an Asian palm civet—a four and a half to eleven pound viverrid (the same family as the catlike genet)—eats a coffee berry. The civet's digestive process infuses the indigestible inner bean with enzymes that give the bean more free amino acids and shorter peptides. When the civet defecates a clump of beans, they are then collected, washed, sun-dried, and roasted. A single cup in an upscale shop can be sold for as high as $35. So next time someone tells you your coffee takes like crap, take it as a compliment.

THE PERFECT MUG

Scientists Klaus Sedlbauer and Herbert Sinnesbichker invented phase change material (PCM), a substance that can absorb, store, and release heat to which it's been exposed. When you initially pour coffee into your PCM cup, the cup will cool it down to the temperature of the given PCM. As the coffee starts to cool by losing heat, the PCM, which just absorbed that heat, releases it back into your cup of coffee.

Perfect . . .

CUP OF TEA

*I*f you've had a sore throat, tough cough, or just a really bad day, a spot of tea is good for what ails you. But not all tea is created equal and, in case you're wondering, anything that you can get in a tea bag doesn't quite measure up to perfection. And if you're British, it's unlikely that an American cup of tea would cut it either.

In 1903, famous British novelist George Orwell, who took his tea quite seriously, wrote an essay detailing his approach to making the perfect cup of tea. In 2003, the Royal Society of Chemistry decided to commemorate the 100-year anniversary of Orwell's essay by publishing his definitive method, originally published in the January 12, 1946 *Evening Standard* newspaper. What this means to you is that the perfect cup of tea is now only a wee bit away, and you don't even have to leave your kitchen. To create Orwell's tea fit for a queen (or king) try the following:

Keep It Fresh

Don't use water that's already been boiled; use fresh. Water that's been boiled before will have lost some of its "dissolved oxygen" and won't maximize your tea's flavor.

Soften Up

Also don't use mineral-laden "hard" water, as the minerals will create "tea scum." If this is the water you have available, use filtered. And by the same token, don't use bottled mineral water to make tea.

Stay Loose

For "perfection," Orwell suggests using loose leaves and a "china or earthenware" teapot. Although tea bags are convenient, they slow down infusion and increase the amount of weighty tannins. It's best to use a ceramic teapot rather than metal because metal can affect the tea's flavor.

Remember That a Little Goes a Long Way

Don't use a lot of tea. One teaspoon per cup is perfect. Tea infusion should take place at as high a temperature as possible. To do this, you need to prewarm your teapot. Fill your pot at least one-quarter full with boiling water and let it stand for thirty seconds. Next, quickly pour the water from the pot, add the tea, and fill with boiled water from the kettle. You should try to synchronize these moves as quickly and smoothly as possible. You want to add the water from the kettle precisely after it has reached a boil. You also can prewarm your teapot in the microwave. Again, fill it a quarter full with water and then heat it for a full minute. Once it's done, pour out the water, add the tea, and then add the boiling water from the kettle. Take the teapot over to the kettle, rather than vice versa.

Time Yourself

In general, brew the tea for three to four minutes. Precise timing will depend on the kind of tea you're using. The idea that the longer you steep the more caffeine is released is a myth, because 80 percent of the caffeine has finished infusing in the first thirty seconds.

Although more time than this is required to release the tannins, which will give the tea some of its flavor and color, after too much time you'll start introducing high molecular weight tannins, which leave a bitter aftertaste. Infusion times vary by type of leaves: Green teas generally need one to two minutes, black teas three to four minutes, and five minutes for chai.

Drink Big

There's no need to drink from a miniature tea cup. The tea will keep its heat longer in a large mug.

Milk It for All It's Worth

If you're going to add milk, add it before you add the tea. Milk proteins will degrade if they encounter temperatures above 167°F. If you pour milk into hot tea, the milk drops separate from the larger volume of milk and come into contact with the high temperature for long enough that the milk proteins will denature, which means the usually-curled proteins unfold and form clumps. While the nutritional content remains, the taste is negatively affected. This isn't as likely to happen when the milk is poured first and the tea next. Fully mixed, the temperature of the tea should be below 165°F.

Add a Spoonful of Sugar

Milk and sugar are a personal preference and fully optional, but the Society notes they work together to counteract some of the tea's natural astringency. Some recent studies suggest milk may also protect the stomach, as there were fewer instances of stomach cancer in cultures that added milk to their tea as opposed to those who drank it black.

Keep It Hot

Between 140°F and 150°F is the perfect temperature at which to drink tea, and the Society says that if its directions are followed, your tea should be in that range within a minute. If the temperature is higher than this, it's too hot for comfort, and you force people to make the socially unforgivable "slurping" sound as they try to cool the tea while sipping it. One way to lower the temperature is to leave a teaspoon in the cup for a few seconds.

So the next time you reach for that old tea bag that's been sitting in your cabinet for years, think again. This is one instance where perfection is as comforting as a cup of hot tea.

Perfect . . .

CUTTING BOARD

*I*f you go to your local home goods store, you'll find a baffling display of cutting boards in the kitchen section. There are cutting boards made of plastic. Cutting boards made of silicon. Cutting boards made of unpronounceable, unidentifiable compounds that promise to combat salmonella and basically cut up your veggies for you.

If you find this aisle overwhelming, relax. The perfect cutting boards are made of wood, so that's what you should buy every time. That's probably not what you've been told, but when the U.S. Department of Agriculture admitted they had no actual science behind their recommendation of plastic cutting boards, Dean Cliver, a professor of food safety at the University of California, saw it was high time for a study. Cliver found that wooden cutting boards have been getting a bad rap. Some of that was intentional sabotage by the rubber industry, he says, when they started pushing plastic and hard rubber boards as more hygienic. Soon the consensus was that wooden cutting boards were less safe and harder to keep clean. Even the FDA maintains that plastic is more bacteria resistant and easier to clean than wood. In his own studies, however, Cliver has found something different.

Cliver found that when knives cut into the surface of plastic cutting boards, tiny cracks "radiate out from the cut," and the bacteria will then settle down into the cracks and just "hang out. They go dormant." While you might kill some 90 percent of these germs by washing, the rest can linger on for weeks. When you put the cutting board in the dishwasher, the bacteria on the surface are just spread around, and the bacteria down in the cracks stay put. Unless your hot water registers over 140°F, he says, the bacteria just aren't going to die.

Cliver's research found that wooden cutting boards absorbed bacteria differently than the plastic boards did. Although the bacteria did get down into the cellulose of the wooden boards, they never resurfaced. He says the researchers were never able to get the bacteria to contaminate knives in later use, so they would not spread to new food. It appears that, once trapped in the wood fibers, the bacteria can't infinitely survive like some slumbering vampire; they will die off eventually. If your wooden cutting board is small enough to fit in the microwave, you can hasten that process by nuking the board for five minutes—although that's essentially a decision of fire danger over bacteria.

In another test, researchers took raw chicken juices and spread them over used plastic and wooden cutting boards. Both boards were then washed with soap and hot water, and dried. Next the researchers cut downward on the boards with knives as if chopping vegetables. No bacteria ever appeared on knives used on the wooden board, but the knives used on the plastic board picked up plenty. No bacteria? Sounds pretty perfect, right?

Go Green

If green-friendliness is a personal prerequisite of perfection, check out bamboo cutting boards or other forms of sustainable wood. "Bamboo-kun" is a naturally occurring antimicrobial agent that exists within the bamboo plant to protect it from fungi.

DATE

*F*orget roses, champagne, and an expensive dinner. According to social psychologist and author Richard J. Crisp, PhD, the perfect date is "on a rollercoaster, sweating, and wearing red." It sounds silly, but it turns out that Crisp's glib summation is rooted in scientific fact.

In a study originally published in 1974 by D. G. Dutton and A. P. Aron, researchers discovered that roller coasters—and other pulse-pounding activities—increase the heart rate and cause shortness of breath and muscle weakness. In reality, these are signs of anxiety. But if they happen on a date, our brains don't necessarily attribute them to the activity. In fact, because these are also some of the same physiological reactions your body has when it's sexually aroused, it seems your brain mistakes the anxiety caused by these adrenaline-fueled activities as being caused by how attracted you are to your date.

These dating activities may also cause you to sweat, which is an important but less critical factor in attraction. Sweat contains pheromones—invisible chemicals that our bodies exude—and these do attract compatible partners of the opposite sex. However, the lure of pheromones is not as insanely strong as any company *selling* pheromones would lead you to believe.

A 1999 study by Randy Thornhill and Steven Gangestad called "The scent of symmetry: A human pheromone that signals fitness?" published in *Evolution and Human Behavior,* finds the time when these chemicals can have a huge impact is while a woman is ovulating. At this time in her cycle a woman tends to prefer men who exhibit greater facial masculinity, who compete with other males for her attention, and have deeper voices. Interestingly, they also found that she's less attracted to her own partner during the time when her fertility is at its peak. But it's not just women whose sex drive is sent into a frenzy by ovulation. Doctor of psychology Jon Maner found that a man's testosterone is significantly boosted when he smells a shirt worn by a woman who is ovulating.

Finally, there's the impact that red can have. It's more than just a sexy color. Dutton and Aron wrote that a woman wearing red "enhances men's attraction." Like the impact of pheromones, this desirability in relation to the color is completely subconscious.

But to step away from science for a moment, Michael Rabby, PhD, an expert in romantic relationships, offers a few other points of perfection: Get sentimental, don't be too rehearsed, be attentive to your date, and do something memorable, like "reciting a famous poem over dinner." Or . . . skydiving. That would take care of the heart-pounding activity. Just slap on some red and you're good to go.

DESTINATION: DATE

A survey conducted by Hotels.com found that 32 percent of women and 46 percent of men think staying in a hotel is the perfect Valentine's Day date. In 2012, *Huffington Post* readers voted Santorini, a Greek Island in the southern Aegean Sea, as the most romantic destination. The runners-up included:

- Buenos Aires, Argentina
- Bora Bora
- Dubrovnik, Croatia
- Halong Bay, Vietnam
- Nevis Island (in the Caribbean Sea)
- Venice, Italy
- Quebec City, Canada
- Santa Barbara, California

. . . and, of course, the City of Lights—Paris, France.

DIAMOND

You may have heard of the "Four C's" of diamonds: cut, color, clarity, and carat. But when you're looking for the perfect diamond, you're not looking at size or color. Instead, the "diamond grading and evaluation appraisal," the grading system used by the Gemological Institute of America to assess diamonds, measures clarity, the word for the overall appearance of a diamond and if it has any blemishes like nicks or chips. This system initially comprised nine grades—steps on the scale of assessment of the diamond, from "flawless" to "imperfect"—but has been modified over the years so that it now is broken down into six categories, with a total of eleven possible grades. A diamond's classification is based on the individual gem's appearance when magnified ten times. The top category, the perfect diamond, is classified as "flawless." Not surprisingly, the rare and perfect flawless-graded diamond is the most valuable; so valuable, in fact, that these flawless diamonds are not the ones typically seen on a ring. A flawless diamond is more likely to be in a museum, but some have shown up at auction. In case you ever find yourself bidding at Christie's with a few extra million dollars, you might want to know the basics of diamond grades.

DIAMOND CATEGORIES AND THEIR GRADES

- **Flawless (FL):** No defects in the surface, called "blemishes," and no internal imperfections, called "inclusions."

- **Internally Flawless (IF):** No inclusions, and on the surface only tiny blemishes.

- **Very, Very Slightly Included (VVS):** Will have extremely tiny inclusions that even for an expert are difficult to see when magnified. The category is broken down into two grades; VVS1 is better than VVS2. Inclusions in this category are too small to be seen by the eye, though in rare cases they may be identifiable in VVS2 diamonds.

- **Very Slightly Included (VS):** Also broken down into two grades, VS1 and VS2. These will have tiny inclusions that are still difficult for an expert to see while under magnification, and generally not visible to the eye, though still, in rare cases, they may be visible in VS2 diamonds.

- **Slightly Included (SI):** Comprising two grades, SI1 and SI2. Inclusions at this level are easily identifiable by an expert when magnified, and may be—but not necessarily—visible to the eye.

- **Included (I):** Three grades, I1, I2, and I3. Inclusions are obvious to an expert when magnified and can also generally be seen by the eye. These inclusions may also compromise the structural integrity of the diamond. Inclusions in I1 can generally be seen by the eye; I2 inclusions are easy to see; and the inclusions in I3 diamonds are so obvious that they can dull the diamond's brilliance and impair the stone's physical integrity.

One perfect, flawless diamond, the Cross of Asia, was discovered in 1902 in South Africa. Originally 280 carats, it was eventually cut down to 79.12 carats to remove all flaws. Another flawless stone, the Star of the Season, sold for $16,548,750 to Saudi Arabian Sheikh Ahmed Fitaihi, and held the record at the time in 1995 for its price before being unseated by the also flawless Wittelsbach-Graff diamond, which sold for 23.4 million. Sheik Fitaihi has received offers to make a profit on Star of the Season, but turned them down. The Wittelsbach-Graff diamond originated in India and once belonged to Philip IV of Spain, and ended up on the royal crown of the King of Bavaria, Maximilian IV Joseph von Wittelsbach. As of 2010, it was on display along with the Hope Diamond at the Smithsonian Institution in Washington, D.C. Sounds pretty perfect, right?

Perfect . . .

DICE

When you bring your own deck to a friendly neighborhood card game and then proceed to win hand after hand, your friends probably won't blacklist you or demand you go with them the next day to get your cards looked at by an expert. (Suckers.) You cannot, however, bring your own set of dice to the Bellagio and expect to start shooting craps.

Given that the casino's business is dependent upon their ability to take more of your money while doling out just enough to keep people coming back, they understand all too well that every Tom, Dick, and Harry would like nothing more than to come in with a pair of dice guaranteed to give them a seven or eleven on their first roll. So in games of chance, the casinos take none.

Casino dice, known as precision or "perfect" dice, are made under the tightest tolerances, assuring that they will be perfect cubes to within a fraction of a millimeter. This guarantees that they have an equal chance of landing on a given side. And if you're thinking that error might be created by how the numbers are put on each side, they've actually covered that, too. When six little holes are drilled on one side of the die for the six, the material they put in (generally white) is precisely equal to the amount of material they took out.

When a casino retires a set of dice, they're marked to show that they're no longer considered playable. In Atlantic City, for example, New Jersey state law mandates a hole be drilled straight through retired dice to stop them from being tampered with and placed back into rotation.

So even if you roll snake eyes, take comfort in the fact that the outcome really has been left to chance.

DOG

*I*f you're looking for the perfect breed of dog, look no further than the wire fox terrier, named for its wire-haired coat. As of 2011, the wire fox terrier as a breed has won Best In Show on thirteen occasions—more times than any other breed—at the annual Westminster Kennel Club Dog Show, the crème de la crème of the show-dog world. Only five individual dogs have won Best In Show more than once, one of them Matford Vic, a wire fox terrier who won in 1915 and 1916.

Bred in England for fox hunting in the seventeenth century, the wire fox terrier is of a size suited to rustling foxes, badgers, and other small game from their holes and hideouts. They're fast, smart, tough, and filled with an insatiable energy. They're also known for their fearlessness, making no distinction between mouse, burglar, or garbage truck. The American Kennel Club (AKC) officially recognized the breed in 1885, and categorizes them as a "Vermin hunter."

But even among the perfect breed, there are those dogs who take that perfection to a whole new level. The characteristics of the wire fox terrier that most perfectly exemplify the breed include the following:

- They should appear alert, and "stand like a cleverly made, short-backed hunter, covering a lot of ground," as the AKC describes the breed on its website.

- They should stand no taller than 15½". The distance from shoulder to the beginning of the tail should be no more than 12", and the length of the head should be 7"–7¼". Its ideal weight is 18 pounds. The measurements of the head should be precisely accurate, but the length of back and shoulder height are approximations, not cut-and-dried rules.

- The length of the foreface, or snout, should be close to the same length as the skull. If the eyes are located too high "up in the skull and too near the ears," it also amounts to a fault, the head being said to have a "foreign appearance." The eyes should not be too prominent, yet "full of fire, life, and intelligence." Ears that hang limp (like a hound's) are undesirable, but even worse is an ear standing partially erect.

- At its widest part, the top of the head should be no more than 3½" in diameter. It should be near to flat but with the slightest slope and become increasingly narrower toward the eyes. A skull wider than 3½" is called "coarse," and if too narrow called "bitchy in head."

- The color of its nose has to be black. The jaws should be strong, and the top and bottom teeth able to close together close to a perfect fit, with the lower canines closing just in front of the uppers.

- Its neck should be graceful, with no sag. The tail shouldn't be docked much more than a quarter of its length. The legs should look straight from any direction, and its thighs should look strong, like "instruments of propulsion."

- The perfect coat will consist of strong hairs growing close together, so that if you tried to spread them apart with your fingers you would not see skin. At its shoulders and neck its coat should be ¾" to 1" long, and elsewhere longer, around 1½". With the exception of "brindle, red, liver or slaty blue," which are considered "serious faults" in a show dog, the colors of a wire fox terrier are generally irrelevant.

- The ultimate test for an individual dog is its form when moving. While in motion, its front legs should swing "like a pendulum," with the power coming from its hind legs. "Perfection of action," they say, comes from the terrier with long thighs and powerful second thighs well angled at the knees, which means the dog has thigh muscles on both the inside and outside of the upper leg.

So if you're looking for the perfect champion pup, go out and get yourself a wire fox terrier. But if you're just looking for some puppy love, head to your local shelter and look for any dog that needs a home.

EAR TO SPEAK INTO

*C*hances are good that, at some point in your life, someone (maybe your grandpa) has said to you, "Talk into my good ear." Interestingly enough, this isn't just based on age. Studies are increasingly showing that the sounds picked up by your right and left ears are processed differently by your brain, and that humans tend to prefer receiving verbal information with the right ear. If the information is presented to both ears at the same time, people will favor the syllables coming in to the right. Scientists have theorized that since most of our linguistic activity occurs in the left side of the brain, input coming in through the right ear is given precedence.

The right hemisphere seems to be predisposed to process negative emotions, and the left, positive emotions. Since the left side of the body corresponds with the right side of the brain, and the right side of the body with the left side of the brain, it's suggested that speaking into someone's right ear puts you in direct communication with the more "agreeable" side.

To test the theory, psychologists Daniele Marzoli and Luca Tommasi of the University G. d'Annunzio in Italy took their study out to the nightclubs of Pescara. The choice of venue, which was guaranteed to be loud, also made it possible to talk selectively into a person's right or left ear without seeming particularly odd. It's what people naturally do in the situation. The question asked was "Do you have a cigarette?" The unwitting study subjects asked in their right ear were twice as likely to produce the cigarette as people receiving the request through their left ear. Their results were published in volume 96 of the journal *Naturwissenschaften*.

RIGHT ON

Studies have found that both people and animals have a tendency to go right when there's something they want: People will turn their heads to the right for a kiss; when toads are going for prey, they attack to the right; and dogs will wag their tails more emphatically toward the right when happy to see their owners. Scientists at the University of Amsterdam found this true in soccer as well; goalies predominantly dove to the right.

Perfect . . .

FACE

*B*eauty may be in the eye of the beholder, but when you're talking about facial symmetry, perfection is definitely possible. Across many studies, facial symmetry repeatedly appears as the most important factor in facial attractiveness. These studies included people of different ethnicities, in different cultures across the world. Symmetry was even valued by babies, who have not yet developed the biases of society; babies gazed longer at a symmetrical face than an asymmetrical one. Facial symmetry is measured by the golden ratio, also called phi, in which two segments have a ratio of 1.618: 1. The golden ratios of a human face involve lines such as the distance between a person's eyes and mouth and the length of the face.

Where you can see this perfection? Just take a look at Elizabeth Taylor. In 2009, psychologist Stephen Link and his colleagues Pamela Pallett and Kang Lee conducted a study of the proportions of ideal faces and applied the golden ratio to Taylor's face. Link found that Taylor "has proportions of those of the ideal."

Working independently, two experts—Nancy Ectoff, author of *Survival of the Prettiest: The Science of Beauty*, and Gettysburg College Professor of Psychology Richard Russell—found that in addition to perfect symmetry, contrast in both features and color also contributed to the perception of beauty. "A higher contrast tends to make the face more feminine," Ectoff explains. In Taylor's case, her pale skin, violet eyes, and dark hair, as well as her full lips and small jaw, were the perfect contrasts.

Facial perfection rules are the same for men, with symmetry, contrast, and masculine features such as a strong jaw, larger noses, and a good forward projection of the face relative to cheek width, consistently scoring high marks in attractiveness. However, when the golden ratio was used to create a formula based on a scale of 1 to 10 for a 2009 *Oprah* show, researchers studying male faces were not able to find a perfect ten, but the face in the top position, with a 9.3, belonged to actor Brad Pitt.

FOREHEAD ENVY

According to the International Society of Aesthetic Plastic Surgery, Elizabeth Taylor is one of the top names given to plastic surgeons by patients seeking a perfect . . . forehead. The other most enviable foreheads belong to Nicole Kidman, Madonna, and Oprah Winfrey. While forehead cosmetic surgery is not one of the top five most popular cosmetic surgeries, injections of a purified protein from the *Clostridium botulinum* bacteria to relax forehead muscles is an extremely popular "tweak" for both men and women.

FLOWER

According to TheRomantic.com, 110 million roses are delivered to lucky women all across America every Valentine's Day. But despite the love for these flowers, are they really considered to be "perfect"?

A perfect flower, by definition, is one that has both male and female reproductive parts. Such a flower is also known as a bisexual flower. The male part of the flower is called the androecium, made up of stamen, which produce pollen. The female part of the flower is called the gynoecium, made up of carpals, which contain ovules. In germination, the pollen fertilizes an ova from the ovules. Perfect flowers reproduce in two different ways. With a complete perfect flower, the dual-sexed plant is either self-pollinated when its stamen releases pollen, which sticks to its stigma and fertilizes its ovary, or has its pollen spread via an insect. With a unisexual perfect flower, only the male or female system actually functions, and is reliant on a flower with the opposite function with which it can reproduce. These unisexual flowers are actually are called "composite" or "incomplete" flowers; an example is the sunflower.

So, is the United States' national floral emblem (the rose) really an example of the "perfect flower"? Rest assured that your Valentine's bouquet truly is perfect, as roses contain both male and female reproductive parts. How romantic!

COMING UP ROSES

The perfect flower, the rose, is also the world's most popular flower. The colors of roses have different meanings. For example:

- Red symbolizes love, passion, romance, and beauty
- Yellow symbolizes friendship and happiness
- White symbolizes purity, unity, and sincerity
- Pink symbolizes gratitude
- Peach-colored symbolizes anticipation
- Blue symbolizes love and prosperity, but has not yet been engineered to exist naturally, and must be made with dyes

So the next time you're looking at flowers, keep these colors in mind. You don't want to send the wrong message.

Perfect . . .

FLUID

*I*n the world of physics, a perfect fluid is an abstract ideal, not something a lab can order through the mail or physically make through clever experiments. This perfect fluid has almost no viscosity, no friction, won't conduct heat, presents no shear stress (the stress a liquid incurs as it moves along a solid boundary), is incompressible, and perfectly follows the laws of fluid mechanics. The real, physical fluids we encounter in everyday life are nothing like this. For example, water, oil, blood, milk, honey, molasses, and chocolate syrup are all fluids, and all with very different characteristics. Additionally, they can all conduct heat by getting warm, and their viscosity changes based on temperature and humidity. Were you to walk through a perfect fluid there would be virtually no resistance—the fluid would not push you in the direction it was flowing. So if you were to run from one side of a pool filled with perfect liquid to the other, it would seem as though there wasn't anything there. Sounds pretty easy compared to making your way through a three-foot-deep pool of honey, right?

Are you picturing a liquid out of science fiction, like *Stargate* or *Star Wars*? Actually some scientists, such as Vladimir Dzhunushaliev, theorize that perfect fluid could exist within wormholes that may (again, theoretically) connect stars. It's important to realize that no one really knows what the perfect fluid would look or feel like or how viscous it would actually be. Viscosity is a liquid's "thickness" or how much resistance it presents. Dominik Steineder at the Institute for Theoretical Physics points out that the record for lowest-viscosity fluid is yet to be set, since his former professor Anton Rebhan has made arguments for the theoretical liquid's possible existence or creation based on calculations of "solving equations from string theory," and applying the "results to the physics of the quark-gluon plasma." Steineder says, "The viscosity depends on several other physical parameters, but it can be lower than the number previously considered to be the absolute lower bound." So, essentially some insanely smart people are experimenting with plasma, which hopefully will make a perfect fluid and *not* suck Earth into some previously unknown wormhole. Theoretically. We'll see how that goes!

ATOM SMASHERS

Researchers at CERN's Large Hadron Collider (LHC) and Brookhaven National Laboratory's Relativistic Heavy Ion Collider (RHIC) collided gold and lead ions at nearly light speed, and for an infinitesimal blink blew the quarks and gluons into independent particles, mimicking the conditions existing within millionths of a second after the big bang. The experiment formed Quark-Gluon Plasma (QGP), which is what researchers are saying is the closest to a perfect fluid they've ever created.

Perfect . . .

FOOTBALL SEASON

*T*he perfect football season occurs when one team wins every single game they play from the first game of the season through to the Super Bowl. An official football season lasts seventeen weeks and begins the weekend after Labor Day every year. There has only been one team in National Football League (NFL) history (starting in 1970 after the NFL and American Football League merged) to have had a complete perfect season: the 1972 Miami Dolphins. Between the fourteen games in the regular season and the three they played in the post-season, they finished 17–0.

The next team to come close to a perfect season was the 2007 New England Patriots, who won all of their games only to lose in the Super Bowl against the New York Giants. That game, Super Bowl XLII, is considered one of the biggest upsets in sports history, and made the Giants the first wild-card team to win the Super Bowl.

The 1935 and 1942 Chicago Bears and the 1948 Cleveland Browns also had perfect seasons, but since it was under the standards of the All-American Football Conference and American Professional Football Association, and thus not under the NFL, they are not counted on that technicality. Too bad, Chicago and Cleveland fans.

PERFECT QUARTERBACK

A quarterback in the NFL is said to have had a "perfect game" if he achieves a perfect passer rating—a number calculated based on passing yardage, completion percentage, interceptions, and touchdowns. The highest official passer rating a quarterback is able to reach is 158.3. To be eligible, the quarterback has to attempt a minimum of ten passes with a minimum 77.5 percent completion rating, have a touchdown pass completion rating of 11.875 percent, a minimum twelve and a half yards for each attempt, and zero interceptions. Recent quarterbacks with perfect passer ratings were Drew Brees in 2009 with the New Orleans Saints and Tom Brady in 2010 with the New England Patriots.

FORGERIES

*S*imilar to a perfect crime, perfect forgeries are those in which the forgeries go undetected, even when looked at closely. Most forgeries can't hold up under close inspection unless they're absolutely perfect. Unfortunately, the Germans were able to achieve this level of perfection when they forged British currency in WWII. Looking for a way to destabilize the British economy during the war, the Germans decided to flood the British market with counterfeit money. In "Operation Bernhard," Jews with expertise in printing and engraving were held in the Sachsenhausen Concentration Camp and forced to produce the notes. The result was described as perfect by numerous sources, including BBC News reporter Sanchia Berg in her 2012 article "Nazi forged bank notes hit sterling confidence, MI5 files show," which said: "On watermarked paper, with elegant copperplate script, and engraving of Britannia, it was a perfect counterfeit."

The initial plan was to drop the counterfeit money from planes, but a plane shortage resulted in the forgeries instead being given to intelligence agents to put in play from the ground. Fortunately, the Bank of England had learned of the plot as early as 1939 from a spy, and the British were able to intercept the shipment in 1943. Only a handful of the forged notes ever made it into circulation within England's borders. Upon seeing the forgeries for the first time, the British were shocked by the quality. In 1945, in a formerly secret file called

MI5, banker Sir Edward Reid described the notes as "a type of forgery so skillful that it is impossible for anyone other than a specially trained expert to detect the difference between them and the genuine notes."

To be safe, The Bank of England withdrew from circulation every banknote £10 and over. But the forgeries were already circulating in other countries, and made it as far as Egypt. The Bank of England was forced to recall all notes under £5 and print new ones, in which they included a metal strip.

By the time Sachsenhausen Concentration Camp was evacuated in April 1945, its printing presses had produced 8,965,080 banknotes for a total value of £134,610,810—translating into roughly $540 million based on the exchange rates of the time. Crates of the forgeries were also dumped from a train carrying the counterfeiters to the Austrian Alps as the Soviets closed in on Berlin. After the war, the notes that still existed in Germany, along with the printing plates, were dumped into Lake Toplitz in the Austrian Alps.

Sometimes perfect isn't all it's cracked up to be.

IS THAT OSCAR A COUNTERFEIT?

Adolf Burger was one of the counterfeiters who survived the concentration camp. He went on to write the book *The Devil's Workshop* and help write the 2007 Austrian film *The Counterfeiters*, which won the 2008 Academy Award for Best Foreign Language Film of the Year.

Perfect . . .

FREE THROW

*D*espite repeatedly making shots that for most would be near to impossible, basketball players given a chance to calmly stand fifteen feet in front of the basket and shoot from the free-throw line with no interference frequently miss their target. In men's college basketball, players miss a little over a full third of their free throws, and in the NBA things improve only slightly, with the professionals missing a quarter of their shots.

After analyzing the trajectories of hundreds of thousands of computer-simulated free throws, Chau Tran and Larry Silverberg, professors at North Carolina State University who also just happen to be mechanical and aerospace engineers, found the perfect shooting angle, rotation speed, and aim necessary for making the basket each time. Rather than going for a swish, Tran and Silverberg recommend that you target the back of the rim, with the goal of leaving a two-inch gap between the back of the rim and ball. The simulations found this would increase the likelihood of a basket by 3 percent. In addition, the ball should be launched, they say, with a backspin of about three hertz, which is a very technical way of saying that the ball should make a full three revolutions on its way to the basket. The backspin has another effect as well, which is to deaden the ball if it comes off the back of the rim or the backboard, giving it a better chance of landing in the basket instead of bouncing off.

You want to develop a consistent release speed, and to do this it's best to make your free throws one smooth body motion, with the ball coming off the middle and index fingers last and projected into the air. As the ball leaves your hand, it should be at an angle of 52 degrees to horizontal, meaning that as the ball travels to the basket, at the highest point in its arc it should be less than two inches below the top of the backboard. As authors Jerry Krause, Don Meyer, and Jerry Meyer explain in *Basketball Skills and Drills*, "For most players, the release angle is too low, which decreases the size of the available target from above." Simply put, they advise to "Shoot up, not out."

And while you may not have your protractor handy during the big game, you can figure out the ideal angle and spin in exactly the way your mother nagged you to master things when you were twelve: practice. Practice makes perfect.

BANK ON IT

The same researchers conducted another study in which they simulated 40,000 bank ("off the glass") and direct shots from 100 different points on the court. They found that within twelve feet of the basket, bank shots are 20 percent more effective than straight shots in the wing areas between the three-point line and the free-throw line, but maintained no advantage when coming from more than twelve feet away located near the free-throw line.

GIFT

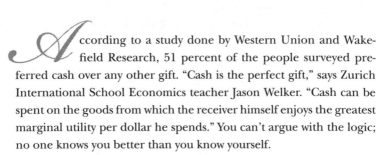

*A*ccording to a study done by Western Union and Wakefield Research, 51 percent of the people surveyed preferred cash over any other gift. "Cash is the perfect gift," says Zurich International School Economics teacher Jason Welker. "Cash can be spent on the goods from which the receiver himself enjoys the greatest marginal utility per dollar he spends." You can't argue with the logic; no one knows you better than you know yourself.

Many people feel that giving cash is impersonal or cold, but if you think about it, it's probably better than clothes that don't fit or kitchen appliances that aren't needed. However, if you still find cash boring, you could always dress it up in creative and funny ways. The "cash tree" with money branches is popular and even practical, as it serves as décor and saves trips to the ATM. Get creative and come up with gamelike ways to give, like inserting rolled bills in balloons before blowing them up. You also can search the Internet for simple tutorial videos on cash origami. Still think cash is crass?

As for how much you should spend on a noncash gift, an organizational psychologist at Stanford University, Francis J. Flynn, and Harvard Business School associate professor Francesca Gino, have now conducted several research studies looking into the psychology of giving and receiving gifts, and their results show that the gifts exchanged are often understood by the giver and receiver quite differently. The researchers found that when people were asked about birthday gifts they had given in the past, their belief was that the recipients' gratitude was proportional to the amount spent. But when people were asked to recall birthday gifts they had received, there was no such correlation. Those having received expensive gifts such as electronic gadgetry or jewelry were *not* significantly more grateful than those who had received gifts of books or T-shirts. The same results were found in a different study by the same researchers, wherein students were asked to imagine giving or receiving an MP3 player or a CD as a graduation present. Those who imagined giving the MP3 player expected a higher level of gratitude from the recipient than did those giving a CD, while the "recipients" were just as grateful for either.

Flynn and Gino believe those findings are due to "egocentric bias," which means that the people doing the giving focus on their own experience and efforts in picking out a gift, but those factors are unknown to the person receiving the gift. If you're weighing an MP3 player against a CD, and end up buying the CD, you may worry about the gift being too insignificant. However, the person receiving the CD will be unaware of the battle you were having and will think the CD is just fine when compared to the alternative of . . . nothing. The same dynamic works in the other direction as well. If you had picked the significantly more expensive gift, the receiver wouldn't be aware of the choice made and thus wouldn't care.

What noncash gifts do receivers appreciate the most? As boring as it may seem, people enjoy receiving things they specifically ask for either personally or through a gift registry. When registries exist and you give a gift not on them, it can backfire, with recipients thinking that you felt you knew their needs better than they do. So if you want to go "off-list," keep it simple—and remember, in the end, the perfect gift is cash!

ONE OF A KIND

If you can't bring yourself to give cash, and are looking for a truly unique gift that can't be replicated at the mall, try websites featuring handmade and vintage goods, like Etsy.com and Artfire.com, where one-of-a-kind pieces can be found in a huge range of prices. Type an interest of the gift recipient in the search field and marvel at the weird and wondrous results.

Perfect . . .

HAND OF POKER

A perfect hand of poker is the term for a hand of cards that a player feels is certain to beat the other players' hands. Tournament player Jim Jackson describes the perfect hand as "a rather strong hand (by far not the best possible poker hand, though) that is made a sure big-time winner by the fact that someone else at the table possess an almost—but not quite—similarly strong hand." Dr. Mark Burtman, another tournament player, similarly describes the perfect hand as "a perfect set of circumstances in which two or more players feel they have a sufficiently good hand to push all their chips into the pot, resulting in disaster for two or more players and profit for another." So part of the difficulty of a perfect hand is that for it to exist, *two or more* players must be convinced they have it as well, convinced enough to put their money and reputation on the line. When the other player goes in, they assume it's a bluff. No one knows who is right until the cards are on the table. Many nonplayers may also know the term "perfect hand" from the 2001 film *Ocean's Eleven* (which was a remake of a 1960 film), in which character Danny Ocean says, "Because the house always wins. Play long enough, you never change the stakes, the house takes you. Unless, when that perfect hand comes along, you bet big, and then you take the house."

While some people might mistakenly define a perfect hand as a royal flush, it's really any hand that gives the holder a clear if not certain advantage to win. A perfect hand is therefore not so much defined by the cards in the hand itself, but by the cards of the opposition it's apt to beat. However, the fact remains that a royal flush is the highest-ranking hand in the game, in which the player holds the ace, king, queen, jack, and ten of the same suit (spades, hearts, diamonds, or clubs). Out of fifty-two cards, there are only four possible royal flushes, so the chances of being dealt a royal flush in a five-card deal are .0015 percent.

The other top hands in poker are, in order of best to worst:

- Straight flush (five successive cards of any same suit)
- Four of a kind (all four being the same number/rank of each suit)
- Full house (three cards of the same rank and a pair of the same rank)
- Flush (five cards of the same suit, of any rank)
- Straight (five cards of any suit, in sequence of rank, with at least two different suits)
- Three of a kind (three cards of any suit of the same rank)
- Two pair (two sets of identical rank but different suits)
- One pair (two cards of the same rank)

A hand with none of these is a high-card or no-card hand, which can still win if you're a master of the bluff, which is pretty perfect in its own right.

P-P-P-POKER FACE

In the July 2010 issue of *PLoS ONE*, Wellesley College psychologist Erik Schlicht published the results of a gambling study in which novice players played poker against a computerized opponent showing various animated faces. The neutral "poker face" didn't unsettle the players nearly as much as the "trustworthy" face did; that expression led to the most folding in its human opponents. Schlicht found this was an "emotional reaction"; that someone appearing trustworthy "must only be betting with good hands."

Perfect . . .

HANDSHAKE

There's evidence humans have been shaking hands for more than 2,500 years, going back to the arm clasp of ancient Rome. According to Professor Geoffrey Beattie, head of psychological sciences at the University of Manchester, the custom can be one of the "most crucial elements of impression formation." Given we only have one chance to make a first "impression formation," it can be useful to be aware of the nuances and method of a perfect handshake.

The major errors people make, Beattie says, are lack of eye contact, limp wrists, sweaty palms, and gripping with too much force. Beattie found that the perfect handshake, which conveys trust and respect to the recipient, is dependent upon twelve factors:

1. Eye contact
2. Pleasant greeting
3. A good smile
4. A complete grip
5. Dry hands
6. The strength of your grip

7. The position of your hand
8. The vigor of the shake
9. The temperature of your hands
10. The texture of your hands
11. An element of control
12. The duration of the shake

The basic gist—for both men and women—is that you move in with your right hand, which should be dry and cool, and then grasp the other person's hand midway in the space between the two of you, with your fingers under the person's palm in a firm grip; again, firm but not so firm that the other person thinks you're trying to overcompensate for something. The handshake itself should be about three mildly vigorous shakes for no more than two to three seconds. All the while, maintain good eye contact and a genuine smile, as you say something socially appropriate and engaging—rather than something really awkward and off-putting.

In addition, body language expert Patti Wood reminds shakers to keep that all-important eye contact to three to five seconds at the maximum. Anything else has a good chance of being perceived as a sexual advance. Awkward!

Perfect . . .

HARDBOILED EGGS

hen looking for the perfect hardboiled egg, you will find an endless number of techniques: Boil them in the water, boil the water first then let them sit, or use eggs fresh from the henhouse. In *The Way to Cook*, Julia Child adapted a hardboiled egg recipe originally written by the Georgia Egg Board. Child describes the perfect hardboiled egg as having a "tender white and yolk set properly. And the perfect hardboiled egg shows not the faintest darkening of yolk where the white encircles it—a most unappetizing chemical reaction . . . caused by too much heat." Another point of perfection is the egg's ability to be neatly peeled. To make the perfect hardboiled egg at home, consider the following tips:

1. Both Child and the Georgia Egg Board recommend using the following: a tall saucepan with a lid, an egg pricker (don't worry if you've never heard of this; they're uncommon) or needle, and a large bowl with ice cubes and water.

2. At the large end of the egg is an air pocket, which will expand as the egg is heated, potentially cracking the egg. Release the air by inserting the pin or egg pricker into the large end of the egg a good quarter of an inch.

3. Lay the eggs in the pan and then fill it with enough water that the eggs are sitting an inch below the surface.

4. Bring the water just to a boil on high heat, then remove the pan from the heat, cover it, and find something else to do for the next seventeen minutes while assuring yourself that anything worth doing is worth doing right.

5. When the seventeen minutes are up, transfer the eggs to the bowl of ice and water and chill them for two minutes. This will shrink the eggs back from inside the shell, making them easier to peel, and you will be less likely to end up with cratered eggs.

6. While the eggs chill, bring the water back to a boil. Call a friend to tell them you're still boiling the eggs.

7. As the water starts boiling again, transfer the eggs from the bowl back to the pan, six at a time.

8. Bring the water back to a boil for ten seconds, which will expand the shell away from the egg, and then return the eggs to the bowl of ice and water, cracking the shells gently in several places.

9. Chill the eggs in the bowl immediately after taking them from the water to keep that verboten dark line from forming around the yolk. If you have the time available, chill them one more time for an additional fifteen to twenty minutes (you'll probably need to add some more ice), which will make the peeling almost effortless. NOTE: If you don't have the time and need to get into your eggs *now*, skip the additional chilling and move right on to the next step.

10. To peel, first tap the egg all around on the edge of the sink, and then under a light stream of running cold water or back in the bowl of ice water, start peeling beginning at the large end. Once peeled, leave the egg to chill in the ice water.

11. Store your eggs in the fridge, either submerged in water or in an open container. They'll keep for two or three days.

This doesn't have the approval of Julia Child or the Georgia Egg Board, but if you're in a rush—and, based on this recipe, maybe you shouldn't be making eggs if you don't have the afternoon free—add a tablespoon of salt and a quarter cup of white vinegar to the boiling water for a batch of eight eggs, to make the shells easier to peel. You won't be able to taste the vinegar and no one will know you took the easy way out.

Perfect . . .

HEIGHT

According to a study led by anthropologist Dr. Boguslaw Pawlowski, as published in *The Daily Mail*, the perfect height for a man is 1.09 times taller than his partner, so a woman who is 5'8" should seek a man who is 6'2". "Females prefer taller men," Dr. Pawlowski states. "Taller men have higher social status, earn more, and are at a lower risk from illness. They also have more reproductive success, as do shorter women. So a male will look for a shorter female." What couple embodies this formula? Victoria and David Beckham, of course. The Beckhams are an almost perfect height match, with Victoria standing at 5'7" and David at 6'0".

In addition, in an American study from the National Bureau of Economic Research, economist Angus Deaton found that people above the national averages in height were happier than shorter people. The average height for men is 5'10", and for women 5'4", indicating that perfect is anything just north of those numbers—in which case, David and Victoria are still "perfect." Deaton attributes the increased happiness to the odd fact that taller people make more money. "Money buys enjoyment and a higher life evaluation," Deaton says bluntly, while somewhere hippies cry. "It buys off stress, anger, worry, and pain. Income is the thing!"

Bestselling author of *The Tipping Point*, Malcolm Gladwell, tackles the issues of height in his 2005 book *Blink: The Power to Think Without Thinking*. Gladwell conducted his own polls of CEOs of *Fortune* 500 companies, and found that "CEOs, as a group, have about three inches on the rest of their sex." Gladwell's findings of these highly-paid men become even more compelling when held up to the fact that only 14.5 percent of U.S. men are 6' or taller. Gladwell points to another study by Timothy Judge, in which Judge stated, "If you take this over the course of a thirty-year career, and compound it, we're talking about a tall person enjoying literally hundreds of thousands of dollars' earning advantage."

Being on either end of height extremes tested poorly with the opposite sex. Men under 5' and over 6'10" and women under 5' and over 6'4" were found the least attractive. In the 2006 study *Height and Reproductive Success*, author R. Scar found that shorter women were more likely to get married than were tall women.

Anthropology indicates that these preferences are strongly influenced by culture. In many non-Western culture studies, researchers discovered that the height of a mate was irrelevant to their subjects. In 2005, David Buss wrote in *The Evolution of Desire* that 80 percent of personal ads requested a man 6' or taller. But that may be only what people *think* they want. In 1979 the *Journal of Personality* reported the results of a study in an article titled "Height and attraction: Do men and women see eye-to-eye?" The researchers, W. Graziano, T. Brothen, and E. Berschied, conducted double-blind studies in which they found that women actually preferred men of medium height—5'9" to 5'11".

Perfect . . .

HIGH HEEL

The perfect high heel is unique for every individual and can be found simply by measuring your foot, says podiatrist Emma Supple. And contrary to what you may think, high heels aren't just for women. Supple explains that heels can be appropriate for men, too, although she understands that men are not likely to wear a heel "no matter how much they might need one." She advises men to try an Oxford or a brogue for a subtle, stylish heel. Why may heels be better? The structures of the feet determine heel height, and Supple insists flats are not always best. To understand why this is so, you first need to know a little bit about the foot's anatomy. Each foot has twenty-eight bones. The talus bone is where the foot connects to the leg, and the sinus tarsi is the recessed area between the talus and the lower leg bone. Supple explains that the sinus tarsi is the key to understanding your ideal heel height.

To properly measure your foot for your perfect heel height, Supple instructs that you sit in a chair and "extend one leg out in front of you," so the leg is parallel with the floor. Relax your foot and ankle so it's not making a tense 90-degree angle, but is at its natural relaxed angle. Draw an imaginary line out from the heel to a point equal to the top of your big toe. Measure the distance from the heel point to the toe point, and you have your ideal heel height. The measurements should form a backwards "L," with the imaginary line being the small, bottom part, and your measurement being the largest part of the "L."

(For some people, like supermodel Kate Moss, that ideal heel height actually is nonexistent and means flats are best.) For most people, "A heel of four and a half inches is fine," Supple told *The Daily Mail* in 2010. "Anything more than that is bad for your posture and makes your bottom jut out and overloads the toes and balls of the feet."

Parisian shoe designer Christian Louboutin spoke to CNN in 2011 about the science behind the construction of his world-famous heels, with their iconic red soles. Denise Richards, Jennifer Lopez, Kim Kardashian, Angelina Jolie—it's a long list of celebrities who think Louboutins are the perfect heel. Fashion writer Garace Doré has publicly admired Louboutin's "craftsmanship." The average price for a pair is $700. "The heel is engineering in itself," Louboutin says. "This little thing that supports the human weight has to have precise balance." Louboutin was always fascinated by dancers, and how they needed to forget about their heels as they danced, and had the "perfect silhouette." Louboutin describes the shoemaking process: He uses models of the human foot, called lasts, to create a balanced shoe. Three parts make up the main shoe: the body, the heel, and the back, which are all sewn together with an inner lining. After the shoe body is created it's left for a week, stapled to a wooden last to "set." Metal stems are inserted into heels of all heights to create perfect balance, and the heel is attached to the shoe while the shoe body is still attached to the last. The last step is polishing and applying the stamp of the golden seal. Other than this info, Louboutin keeps his shoemaking secrets to himself. He quipped to CNN, in his thick French accent: "I'm designing shoes, and sometimes people are pretty addict, you know, it's an addiction in a way. So curing that, I feel a bit like a doctor. And a doctor has professional secrets."

Supple, the actual doctor, is less secretive, and warns that heels are definitely too high when the wearer is "teetering on [her or his] tiptoes." She is strongly against heels that feel like "self-torture." Avoiding shoes like that may seem obvious, but check out the wobbles on the women leaving a club at 2:00 A.M. It's not just because of the drinks.

HOMEMADE FRENCH FRIES

*B*y 2004, almost forty years after McDonald's stopped serving fresh-cut potatoes, nearly a third of the entire potato crop produced in the United States is turned into frozen French fries. We've become so accustomed to frozen fries we're somewhat shocked or impressed when someone claims they make their own. However, celebrity chef Bobby Flay has a different opinion about what makes the perfect homemade French fry.

An Iron Chef on *Iron Chef America*, the host of nine cooking shows, and the chef/co-owner for New York's Mesa Grill and Bolo, Flay put out a cookbook named after a classic American trio—*Burgers, Fries, and Shakes*. To achieve the perfect fries at home, try this Flay-inspired recipe:

The Perfect Homemade Fries

YIELD: FOUR SERVINGS

Five big russet potatoes. NOTE: Choosing the right potatoes is important. A professor of Food Chemistry at Rutgers University, Karen Schaich, warns you're better off making mashed potatoes if the ones you have are soft. Make sure to pick a high-density potato like a Russet Burbank, Schaich advises, because when you try to fry a soft potato it will absorb the oil, which eliminates any chance of the potatoes becoming crispy, resulting instead in mushy, oil-soaked fries.

One quart of peanut oil (peanut oil is perfect due to its high boiling point)

Kosher salt

1. Either peel or simply wash the potatoes, depending on whether you want the skin. Cut them into ¼"-thick slices lengthwise; then cut the slices, again lengthwise, into ¼"-thick fries. Place them in a large bowl filled with cold water, and put the bowl in the fridge for one to eight hours.

2. If you have a deep fryer, go ahead and use it to cook the fries; otherwise, use a heavy-bottomed stock pot. Heat the oil to 325°F. Line a baking sheet with paper towels.

3. Take your bowl of fries out of the fridge and drain the water. Pat the fries dry with paper towels in manageable batches. Cook each batch in the oil for three to four minutes, turning frequently. Once the fries go limp and have turned a pale blond color, remove

them with a mesh strainer basket or skimmer and place them on the paper towel–lined baking sheet.

4. After all of the potatoes have been cooked, raise the temperature of the oil to 375°F. Again in batches and turning frequently, refry the potatoes for three to four minutes, and remove when golden brown. Place the batches on fresh paper towels, salt, and serve! NOTE: Food writer Kelly Dobkin recommends briefly blanching the chilled fries in boiling water before you double fry to achieve the "perfect creamy interior and crunchy exterior."

Don't be frustrated if your homemade fries don't look or maybe even taste as "perfect" as those made in a commercial fryer, as those machines remove some of the human error factor by using oil at its best stage, and with greater volume comes the ability to recycle oil at its peak before it degrades. Homemade still gives you the advantage of fresh fries over frozen, and the ability to choose your own spuds (like organic), so once you get the hang of it, you might never go back to commercial!

JAMES BOND

An interesting thing goes on when we read books. Assuming there are no pictures of the fictional characters within the book or on the cover, we rely on the author's descriptions. But of the millions of people who read *The Adventures of Tom Sawyer*, despite Mark Twain's description of Tom Sawyer, are they all seeing the same Southern young man in their imaginations? If we were put in a room and presented with a "Tom Sawyer line-up," would we all pick the same one? And even if we all did, would it be the same "Tom Sawyer" that Twain would pick if he were in there with us?

And then the movie comes out, and everyone suffers some sort of disillusionment. "I can't believe they chose him, of all people." "He doesn't look like that in the book, I'm sure of it." Much of this is because facial expressions have some leeway. Sure, we can tell both people are "smiling," but is it the same exact smile?

As of 2012, there have been twenty-three James Bond movies, starring seven different actors. With each new face, a debate ensues about who has been the best. But back in 1962, when the film *Dr. No* came out, Ian Fleming had already been writing Bond books for ten years. The author had an idea of who James Bond was, and had commissioned an artist to draw an image of Bond, like a crime sketch, before there was ever talk of a film. The artist decided Fleming's

Bond was a looking a little too antiquated, and reworked the image to give him a more of a rugged look.

Prior to *Dr. No*, Fleming drew up a list of actors he thought could play the role:

- Cary Grant
- David Niven
- James Mason
- Patrick McGoohan
- Rex Harrison
- Richard Burton
- Stewart Granger

In 2007, Professor Richard Wiseman from the University of Hertfordshire and Rob Jenkins from the University of Glasgow used a technique of blending faces called "prototyping" to merge the faces of the actors on Fleming's list in order to come up with a face that had the characteristics of all of them. They ended up with someone who the researchers say most resembles . . . Sean Connery, who actually ended up starring in *Dr. No*. According to Jenkins, "Sean Connery comes out of it quite well." In fact, Connery significantly influenced the on-screen character of Bond, who up to this point hadn't been witty, and certainly not Scottish.

Never seen *Dr. No*? Plop down on your couch with a martini (shaken, not stirred, of course) and watch the perfect Bond . . . James Bond . . . in action!

REQUEST DENIED

Ian Fleming's first choice to portray James Bond was Cary Grant. Why would the first choice of the very creator of the character not be used? At the time, the studio making the film couldn't afford Grant's salary.

JOKE

Obviously, humor is about as subjective as anything can be, so defining the "perfect joke" is like defining any other theoretical concept. However, there are various factors identified as being successful to this specific form of comedy, as psychology professor Richard Wiseman has found. According to his studies, a perfect gag requires three factors:

1. Anxiety
2. A feeling of superiority
3. The element of surprise

The key to understanding what really makes a joke "work" lies within the nonsensical jokes of children. Have you ever been told by a 4-year-old that there's a "frog on your head" or some similar silliness? Well, based on these jokes, University of Colorado psychologists A. Peter McGraw and Caleb Warren believe their research hits on what it is we think is funny, and they've termed it "benign immorality." Four-year-olds aren't able to grasp this concept, and they fail when they attempt a joke with the nonsensical "humor" (in their estimation) of the frog-on-the-head bit, but they completely innocently, unintentionally *succeed* with a joke when simply and earnestly speaking blunt truth in situations requiring tactful and nuanced language.

Previous theories have held that comedy works due to incongruity, or when we feel a sense of superiority; Freud thought it was a release of tension. However, as McGraw and Warren point out, killing your spouse might fall under each of those, but most people wouldn't find it funny. They believe the key to what we find humorous lies in a situation in which society's rules are violated, but only when we feel it has been done safely.

To illustrate benign immorality in its simplest form, they offer the example of the Three Stooges. The Stooges do things to each other that constantly violate what we know is the right way to behave, but because it's wildly unreal, it can be funny. As an experiment, McGraw and Warren presented subjects with situations of potential humor. In one, there are two scenarios in which Jimmy Dean is looking for a new spokesman for his pork products. In one version a rabbi is hired, and in another a farmer. Surprisingly, the rabbi, who has to keep kosher, speaking for and promoting a company that sells pork products— which is as far as you can get from kosher—came across as funny, while the version with the farmer did not. This basis for humor can also explain why some people don't find things funny. It's quite possible that religious Jews may not have found the rabbi joke funny, because it wouldn't feel "safe."

Safely violating society's rules as comedy does seem to be reflected in our popular culture, as it describes the majority of television sitcom jokes as well; we see from some of the yawn-worthy laugh-tracked jokes, there is such a thing as "playing it too safe."

Perfect . . .

KISS

*T*he perfect drug? The perfect kiss. Over the years, scientists have found that a great kiss releases a whole host of endorphins whose combined impact is more powerful than morphine. Adrenaline causes excitement; oxytocin causes bonding; and the feel-good trio of dopamine, serotonin, and norepinephrine causes pleasure. But, to be "perfect," there are some criteria that the kiss has to meet.

To begin with, the kiss has to connect on several levels. Let's start with the basics. First, it's critical to maintain good hygiene, as that will eliminate most of the elementary potential turnoffs. Brush and floss twice a day to avoid plaque buildup that can cause bad breath. To improve your breath between brushings, carry gum or mints so you can ensure a fresh-smelling mouth.

To release the oxytocin, a level of trust and comfort is required, so try to avoid nonromantic environments and uncomfortable positions, and be mindful of your partner's comfort cues. The most common kiss complaints are that they're too wet or include too much (or too little) tongue. These issues can easily be adjusted depending on what turns your partner off . . . or on. Great love is always buoyed by great communication.

The next step is to get into what Rutgers Professor of Anthropology Dr. Helen Fisher calls "a novel situation" to stimulate the release of the chemical pleasure trio. This could be a new partner, a new situation, or even just a new kissing technique. This doesn't mean you have to re-create Spider-Man and Mary Jane's upside-down kiss in the rain to feel the rush with a longtime partner . . . but it wouldn't hurt. Thankfully, *The Kama Sutra* features thirty different kissing techniques to help you find some new material without having to get superacrobatic or find a new partner.

In addition, sexologist Ava Cadell, PhD, suggests adding sensory augmentations like mint lip balm to bring a level of perfection to a kiss. "Menthol triggers the body's cold receptors," Cadell explains. "And when that's combined with your warm breath, you'll get a tingly sensation from your lips straight down to your genitals." Wow! Other possibilities for stimulating the senses include drinking champagne (for the bubbles, naturally), and enjoying strawberries together, as the berries activate the sweetness receptors in the mouth for a pleasant alteration in taste perception.

Also, if you're looking for that "whoosh," try to squelch any stress that you may be feeling. Thanks to the stress hormone cortisol, having your breath taken away by a kiss while you're stressed is impossible, since cortisol inhibits vasodilation and that rush of increased blood flow. So, do your best to release negative anxiety, forget the outside world, and get lost in that "oh-so-perfect" moment.

FRANKLY, MY DEAR

"No, I don't think I will kiss you, although you need kissing badly. You should be kissed and often. By someone who knows how," Rhett Butler famously told Scarlett O'Hara in the 1939 film *Gone with the Wind*. According to a poll by ABC News and *People* magazine, Rhett and Scarlett win "Top Movie Kiss," as voted by film fans. Second place went to 1953's *From Here to Eternity*, with another iconic, famous kiss—in the crashing waves on the beach, with Burt Lancaster and Deborah Kerr.

Perfect . . .

MARTINI

*T*echnically, in the world of liquor consumption, a "perfect" martini is a gin martini with equal parts dry and sweet vermouth, garnished with a cherry. But when it comes to perfect as in "best," a little friendly—and fierce—competition ensues.

On November 19, 2002, six of New York City's best bartenders were invited to a martini-off: Shinichi Ikeda from Angel's Share, Del Pedro from Grange Hall, Sasha Petraske from Milk & Honey, Rhino from Chateau, Albert Trummer from Town, and Jason Woodruff from Joe Allen. Dale "King Cocktail" DeGroff, Gary "Cocktailian" Regan, and Lowell "Dr." Edmunds sat in judgment. The last martini standing belonged to Albert Trummer.

Food and beverage writer Frederic Koeppel referred to Albert Trummer's "almost pharmaceutical approach to making a drink." Indeed, Trummer's reputation as a "bar chef" far exceeds the traditional bartender. His perfect martini has been featured in a variety of media, including *Esquire* and Fox News.

Trummer's Martini

Cracked ice

1 ounce dry vermouth (Noilly Prat, preferably)

4 ounces ninety-four proof gin
(Bombay Sapphire, Beefeater, or Tanqueray)

1 olive (for garnish)

1. Fill a shaker with cracked ice, pour in dry vermouth, give it a quick stir, and then strain out and discard the vermouth.

2. Add gin. Give it a quick stir of ten seconds.

3. Strain it into a cocktail glass that's been chilled, and add an olive for garnish.

Perfect . . .

MOVIE

A perfect movie is *Back to the Future*. That's no shock to anyone still waiting around for their chance to buy a hoverboard. But besides coveting the dream-tech, the adventure, and Christopher Lloyd's wildly enthusiastic line deliveries, once again, there's actual science to support its perfection.

Researchers from Cornell University, lead by psychologist James Cutting, undertook a study in which they measured the duration of each shot in every scene of 150 of the most popular movies released between 1935 and 2005. The movies spanned five genres: drama, comedy, animation, adventure, and action. Using the kind of math that would numb most of our brains, they took the series of shot lengths and transformed them into "waves" for each film. They were looking for the 1/f fluctuation.

In chaos theory, the 1/f fluctuation is a constant in the universe, somewhat analogous to the idea of the golden ratio that runs through everything—in nature, music, engineering, economics, and as a pattern of attention taking place in our minds. It is a rhythm, often undetectable in the surrounding chaos. And yes, they went looking for it in Hollywood and found it there, too. The study found that films made after 1980 approached the universal constant more consistently than those made earlier. This suggests that over the years, the sequence of shots chosen by the directors, editors, and cinematographers has been coming increasingly closer to matching our natural attention pattern. That would help explain why movies made more recently have a much more natural and realistic feel than those of the past, making newer movies easier to identify with and allow for our suspension of disbelief as we watch them.

The researchers suggest that filmmakers most likely have *not* been consciously crafting their movies with this in mind. What is perhaps more plausible is that a form of natural selection has been taking place in the movies, as the public came to appreciate and enjoy certain rhythms and shot sequences over others. As people examined what was successful, these examples were then taught to other filmmakers, and the shift began within the industry.

The genre that comes the closest to consistently matching the 1/f pattern is action, with adventure, animation, comedy, and drama following in order. Individual movies in each genre have come close to almost perfect 1/f rhythms. Despite being made years ago, 1955's *Rebel Without a Cause* and Hitchcock's *The 39 Steps* from 1935 matched the rhythm, as did the more recent *The Perfect Storm* in 2000.

Wait a minute, Doc. Back to *Back to the Future*. Naturally, the 1985 film scored high in Cutting's study with its 1/f rhythms; in fact, Cutting describes the film's 1/f rhythms as "near ideal." But the other reasons we like it can be found in any film textbook, such as *Storytelling in the New Hollywood* by Kristin Thompson: traditional three-act structure, a hero's journey, plot, story, setting, characters, tension, stakes, reveals, and of course, a happy ending. These popular elements, done exceptionally well, usually leave a devoted audience. Throw in the proper rhythm and *perfecto*!

GOLDEN RATIO

The golden ratio is 1.61803399. It is a ratio of distances. A rectangle, for example, in which the ratio of the long side to the short side matches the golden ratio is said to be more visually pleasing than ones that don't. Beginning in the Renaissance, artists and architects frequently tried to incorporate the ratio into their projects.

NIGHT'S SLEEP

For the average, healthy adult, a perfect night's sleep, where one wakes up feeling good and refreshed, is attainable with proper "sleep hygiene." If you've never experienced insomnia, surely you lead a charmed life. If you have chronic insomnia, you probably already know you should be talking to your doctor (because if your insomnia is caused by sleep apnea or hypertension, this tips aren't likely to help, but your doc can). And if you're self-medicating with booze and sleeping pills, stop now! Fortunately, there are a few safe, chemical-free steps to take to usher in sleep and to help you sleep well.

Cycle It

As Dr. David Kantra reported in the March 2010 issue of *PsychDigest*, humans sleep in ninety-minute cycles. Picture each cycle as a "V," string the V's together, and you get a graph of sleep. It takes forty-five minutes to get from the base to the top of the V and then another forty-five minutes to get back down to the base, for a total of ninety minutes. If your alarm goes off in the morning in the middle of a V, it will be very difficult to wake up. Kantra advises that you try to time your sleep by estimating your fall-asleep time and then scheduling your wake-up time accordingly, in multiples of the superimportant ninety-minute cycles.

Wind Down

A 2012 survey with British bedding brand Bedeck (say *that* five times fast) revealed that two hours of wind-down time before bed is ideal, and seemed to be enhanced by spending twenty of those minutes in pajamas. Alcohol disrupts the first stage of sleep, so skip the nightcap.

Set the Scene

In feng shui, dark and bright pinks and purples are high-vibration colors of the "fire" variety, and thus are overstimulating sheet colors. Sheets in the wide color range of human skin tones are considered the most soothing. Prefer hard science? Avoid blue light. Dr. Simon Archer of the Surrey Sleep Research Centre explains: "Any light suppresses the hormone melatonin, which peaks during the night to make you feel sleepy. But it's actually blue-light receptors in the eye that are responsible for that, so red light will help you sleep better." It would take a bit of engineering with colored bulbs, but a bedroom with red lights at night and blue lights in the morning is ideal.

Have a Healthy Bite

In his book *The Four Hour Body*, Tim Ferriss advises having "two tablespoons of almond butter on celery sticks," before bed to ensure that low blood sugar doesn't get the best of your sleep. Ferriss also adds flaxseed oil "to further increase cell repair during sleep and thus reduce fatigue."

Turn Off Your Brain

Try a sleep hypnosis audio program. Plenty are free online, or you can try Hypno-Peripheral Processing by Dr. Lloyd Glauberman, in which two stories are told at the same time, for "gentle sensory overload," as Glauberman calls it. "Eventually," Glauberman says, "it becomes fatiguing to listen to, and your conscious mind drifts away."

So stop counting sheep and start getting the perfect night's sleep!

NUMBER OF CHILDREN
TO HAVE

*Y*ou may have heard of studies proclaiming that the average family has 2.5 kids or that it doesn't matter how many kids you have as long as you keep it to an even number so no one feels left out. But it's time for these myths (and impossibilities) to give way to simple science. As published in the journal *Social Science and Medicine*, researchers in Norway looking at the birth and death records of 1.5 million men and women discovered that for the healthiest balance between stress and rewards, the perfect number of children to have is two. People who didn't have children, along with those who had only one, had a higher risk of death from illnesses such as lung complications, alcohol abuse, and heart disease, while parents with more than two children experienced a combination of both positive and negative health issues. Researchers suggest that the latter could easily be due to the increase in both the emotional and financial stress of maintaining more people.

And if that wasn't bad enough, parents with more than four children simply have a higher risk of dying, with mothers four times as likely to die from cervical cancer, whereas the fathers of four or more were more likely to meet accidental and violent deaths. The only health benefit found in these mothers was the added protection against breast cancer a woman acquires from the changes her body undergoes during pregnancy. Furthermore, the study found a drop in happiness when more than four children were in the home.

So for health and happiness, two children are pretty much perfect. Plus, no one will get left out and the extra room in the back seat will cut down on the pinching battles that you may remember from your own childhood. Sounds a lot like perfection, right?

NUMBER OF HOURS
TO SLEEP

*T*he perfect number of hours to sleep is just what you've always heard: eight. Precisely how many hours of sleep adults need to function at their best has always been a contentious issue, but a significant sleep-deprivation study in 2003 by David Dinges, head of the University of Pennsylvania's Sleep and Chronobiology Lab, supports the eight-hour convention.

For two weeks in the lab, Dinges had subjects divided into three groups assigned to sleep for four-, six-, or eight-hour periods. Every two hours, participants were given a psychomotor vigilance task to gauge their sleepiness and ability to maintain sustained periods of attention. The task required subjects to sit in front of a computer for ten minutes and press the space bar each time numbers, which were set at random intervals, flashed on the screen.

A number of tasks you perform over the course of the day require sustained attention, and when you suffer "microsleeps" as short as half a second, you can end up doing things like rereading sentences, you can end up doing things like rereading sentences (gotcha!) or barreling into a bumper that's stopped in front of you at a red light.

For the two weeks of the study, those who slept for eight hours showed no deterioration in cognitive skills and almost no attention lapses. But both the four-hour and six-hour groups began a steep decline, which worsened with each passing day. Toward the end of the first week, a quarter of those in the six-hour group failed to stay awake at the computer, and at the end of the second week they were having five times as many lapses as they did on their starting day. Predictably, the four-hour group performed the poorest, but the six-hour group also struggled significantly. Dinges found them comparable to a previous study in which subjects stayed awake for twenty-four hours. In both cases of the four- *and* six-hour groups, the end of the study found the subjects with the cognitive function of a legally drunk person.

If eight hours is good, you might think that nine hours is better. But in another study done by Dinges's colleague Gregory Belenky, study subjects who got nine hours of sleep performed the same as those with eight. Of course, like most averages, there is a bell curve, and a small population on either side is genetically predisposed to function at their best with fewer or more than eight hours.

TIME TO SLEEP WHEN TIME IS SHORT

Is there a perfect time of day in which to sleep? According to a Stanford University sleep study, there is. Subjects were divided into two groups: The first group slept from 10:30 P.M. to 2:30 A.M., and the second slept from 2:15 A.M. to 6:15 A.M. After a week of deprivation, everyone's abilities had been compromised, but those in the group with the early-morning sleep shift from 2:15 A.M. to 6:15 A.M. performed significantly better.

OLYMPIC GYMNASTIC "10"

*I*n a sport where medals are won and lost by tenths of a point, the pursuit of perfection starts at an early age. Traditionally in gymnastics, since the 1924 Olympics, the perfect score was a 10.00. Gymnastic scoring would actually start with a fixed score—8.4 for men, 8.8 for women. Points would then be deducted or added depending on mistakes and difficulty of moves, based on the International Gymnastics Association's Code of Points.

At the 1976 Summer Olympic Games in Montreal, fourteen-year-old Nadia Comaneci earned the first-ever 10.00 in Olympic gymnastics for her routine on the uneven bars. The degree to which this was unexpected was highlighted by the scoreboards, which had to report them as 1.0 since they weren't even capable of displaying a numeric 10.00. The crowd and Comaneci herself were confused until the announcement was made: "Ladies and gentlemen, for the first time in Olympic history, Nadia Comaneci has received the score of a perfect ten." And the crowd went wild.

Nadia's "first" perfect 10 was actually only the first under the standards of the International Gymnastics Federation (FIC). France's Albert Séguin scored the first recorded 10.00 in the 1924 Summer Olympics in Paris, France, on the side vault. At the same event, twenty-four men scored a perfect 10 for the now defunct rope-climbing competition.

However, in 2008 the perfect 10 was eliminated when the scoring system was overhauled. The FIC's reason for the change is that it is searching for a "more perfect" perfect. The new system involves an "A" score, based on number of completed moves and difficulty, and a "B" score, based on artistic impression, with no maximum.

Although the new system might prove to be fairer, fans mourn the perfect 10 system, which had been utilized for about eighty years. "It's so hard to define a sport like ours and we had something unique," Comaneci laments. "The 10.00, it was our first and now you give it away." American 10.00 recipient Mary Lou Retton agreed that the new system is "more confusing for fans" and athletes alike. The routines now may inch toward more technical perfection, but it's uncertain how much fans will care about minor details without the historic and rousing "10.00" display. Maybe the quest for perfection isn't so perfect after all.

DISSECTING PERFECTION

Applying the same technology often used to give animated characters lifelike movements, biomechanists at the University of Delaware have been helping figure skaters perfect their routines. Ceiling cameras record the movements of forty-two markers placed on a skater's body, and 3-D images are later made that both skater and coach can manipulate to understand how specific movements can be improved, and even to create virtual scenarios so they can visualize "what could be."

PAC-MAN GAME

*I*f you're not a gamer you may not realize it, but there is such a thing as a perfect Pac-Man game, which is what it's called when a player reaches level 255 without missing a single dot, pellet, ghost, or fruit, and doesn't lose a single life. The maximum possible score is 3,333,360 points. When a player reaches that score and that level, a glitch splits the screen and the game becomes unplayable.

While many claimed to have achieved the perfect score, the first person to be verified doing so (by Twin Galaxies International Scoreboard) was Billy Mitchell on July 3, 1999, at the Funspot Family Fun Center in Laconia, New Hampshire. The feat took about six hours, and as Mitchell didn't lose any lives (you earn backup "lives" within the game, so one death is often not the end of the game), it only required one quarter. Mitchell was thirty-three years old at the time, meaning he was fourteen when the game was released in 1980.

Many video-game fans made claims they could beat the split-screen level, but when their boasts were brought to the test, they all failed. Mitchell himself offered $100,000 to anyone who could beat the split screen by January 1, 2000, but the prize went unclaimed as the task soon proved impossible.

However, in 2009, the sixth person to ever attain a perfect score, David Race, did so in three hours, forty-one minutes, twenty seconds

(3:41:20), a new record. Race was forty years old at the time, so he was eleven years old at the time of the game's release. In 2010, Race lost the record to Chris Ayra, then Rick Fothergill, and then subsequently won it back with a time of 3:34:08; Twin Galaxies once again verified the score. Race then beat his own high score again on January 4, 2012, with a total time of 3:33:1.4. Race told Examiner.com that his goal was "to simply achieve a perfect game."

"I had a notion it was something pretty big in the classic gaming world," Race said modestly, right before he gave his fellow perfect-gamers their due. Race also thanked Don Hodges for developing the winning technique, called "ninth key pattern" (for tutorials on this pattern, search *www.youtube.com* for "Pacman 9th Key Pattern"), as well as his late father, his girlfriend, her children, and his children. So we can either assume that in between all that game perfecting he still managed time for family or he was simply thanking them for putting up with him.

@*!# MAN

Pac-Man was developed in Japan, and was originally going to be called "Puck-Man" in the United States. (The original Japanese name was Pakkuman.) But it was soon decided "Puck-Man" was too easily defaced into every youth's favorite F-word, so it was instead modified to "Pac-Man."

Perfect . . .

PAIR OF JEANS

*E*veryone knows that a good pair of jeans can be hard to find. While most women are open with this complaint, even fashion-shy men will usually 'fess up to being frustrated by shopping for jeans. In a 2012 article in the UK's online version of the paper *The Sun*, writer David Firth said: "If you're a man, you wear jeans. Simple really." Firth then described shopping for jeans as "a nightmare." But according to *Vogue*, if money doesn't matter the perfect pair of jeans comes from 3x1 denim boutique in New York City. Sure, there are endless style guides to inform you how to pick the best fit for your body type, but why bother when you can get a pair made specifically not for your "type," but for your actual body?

Vogue's sentiments are echoed by many, including fashion site Refinery29.com, whose writer Kristian Laliberte enthused, "We've needed the perfect pair of summer jeans, and obviously, we finally found 'em." *Huffington Post* writer Brooke Bob hailed the 3x1 jeans as the "priceless perfect fit." It's not surprising that 3x1 is the favorite of top fashionistas. Founder Scott Morrison has a reputation for high-end denim with his companies Paper Denim and Cloth, and Earnestly Sewn. He was featured in *Fox Business*, in which writer Lauren Covello states, "Morrison wanted to return to the early days of jeans making, when things were more or less done by hand . . . He wanted to create

123

something special." And creating something special—perfect, in fact—is exactly what Morrison did.

3x1 features different levels of customization. For $525– $750, clients can pick their own fabric and hardware from a staggering array of options in the store/warehouse/factory, and the jeans are sewn on-premises. (Even the majority of as-American-as-apple-pie Levis are now produced overseas.) For the 100 percent customized experience, clients including celebrities and athletes are cracking their wallets open to the tune of $1,200—the *starting price*—for what is known as "bespoke denim." Every aspect of these bespoke denim wonders is tailored to the individual, from fabrics sourced around the world to the ideal, flattering cut for a specific body to carefully engineered stitching that creates a particular look—like longer legs, a lifted butt, or slimmer hips. One tailor handles the whole process for each order, so the client is aware of the entire artistic and technical process behind the creation.

If you're still sputtering from that over-the-top price tag, then Civali will soon have your perfect pair. This company first made a stir online with its Kickstarter.com campaign, in which the public backs a specific project for rewards. The public seemed to like the company's idea of offering custom-fit jeans at a mere $60. Soon the "Backers," as Kickstarter officially calls contributors, pledged funds from around the world to the Chicago-based jeans company. With their help, Civali blasted past its initial fundraising goals and is now moving toward full production.

The brainchild of Elmhurst College senior Leona Liu and recent University of Denver grad Sam Miller, Civali's Kickstarter page states, "The price of jeans has gotten out of control." It goes on to explain Liu and Miller's quest to find a way to produce custom jeans at a reasonable price—including a trip to China to check out the popular manufacturing options. After much research, they found a combination of Autocad software for customizing the pieces per a client's measurements, and a cutting machine to cut down on time-intensive, expensive labor.

The Civali Kickstarter page cleverly notes: "In this day and age, we have the ability to clone cattle, smash atoms together, and create antimatter, but when it comes to finding a pair of jeans that fits perfectly . . . good luck!" Civali's tenacity to find a cheaper custom fit is indeed good luck for the consumer. Unless, of course, a wad of twelve hundred bucks is just burning a hole in your pocket.

PALATE

A perfect palate would be one with as many taste buds as possible, to catch as many flavor nuances in any given subject. A critic may argue there's no such thing as a "perfect" palate, as too many taste buds may make someone too sensitive, but many people consider "supertasters"—who have more taste buds than the rest of the population—to have perfect palates. About a quarter of the population are supertasters, with higher concentrations in the demographics of women, Asians, and Africans. Another 25 percent of the population falls into the category of "nontasters"—people with fewer taste buds than average.

Supertasters are touted as having perfect palates for the purpose of being professional tasters of food, candy, coffees, and wine. Some professional tasters taste grocery-store food for consistency and quality. Their earnings begin at $30,000 a year, but with training and a proven track record for excellence, one can become an executive and make over $100,000. Jennifer Koen is a taster for Godiva chocolates, and was trained by the company as well as graduating from a "chocolate school" in Montreal. Koen conducts visual, smell, and taste tests on the chocolates, taking tiny bites she is careful to push to all taste buds. Other tasters chew and spit out the food after tasting.

The director of Chapman University's Sensory Evaluation Laboratory, Fred Caporasco, does acknowledge that tasters are "trained, just like you train athletes," and that professional tasting isn't a career for every supertaster, as a supersensitive palate will pick up "these little nuances in the product the average consumer can't detect."

Want to know if you have a "perfect palate"? A supertaster can be easily identified. Beverly J. Tepper, a Rutgers University food science professor, dots small pieces of paper with a bitter compound called 6-n-propylthiouracil (PROP), and passes it out for her students to taste. The supertasters are immediately apparent, with their disgusted reaction. The rest of the class looks around, confused, because they taste only paper.

Roland Fisher was actually first to discover the supertaster-finding power of PROP, in the 1960s. Prior to that, DuPont chemist A. L. Fox was seeking out supertasters in the 1930s with phenylthiocarbamide (PTC), a bitter (if you can taste it) yellow powder that doesn't actually exist in food. The ability to taste was attributed to a genotype called TAS2R38. PTC also has some interesting demographics, with only 58 percent of indigenous Australians able to taste it but 98 percent of indigenous North, South, and Central Americans able to do so, in what was determined to be a dominant genetic trait.

Tepper's research led to some remarkable discoveries in terms of supertasting and lifestyle. Examining a group of women in their forties, Tepper found supertasters have a lower body mass index (BMI) than "regular"-palated people, and nontasters had the highest BMI, due to a preference for fatty and sugary foods. A 2005 study coauthored by experimental psychologist Linda Bartoshuk found that supertasters were at a greater risk for colon cancer, most likely due to their heightened palate giving them an aversion to vegetables. (But before you decide that makes you a supertaster, bear in mind they also may have an aversion to the strong tastes of alcohol and coffee.)

Perfect . . .

PENALTY KICK

$\mathscr{P}$enalty kicks in soccer are awarded to a team based on a foul committed by the opposing team. A kicker is given a chance to take a direct kick toward the goal (with the goalie present) from a distance of twelve yards away. According to research from Liverpool's John Moores University, a perfect penalty kick in soccer is the result of a ball kicked with precision to the right or left of the goalie, aimed high, and traveling with a velocity between 56 and 64 miles per hour. Speeds below 56 mph increased the possibility of interception by the goalie, while speeds above 64 mph increased the odds of an inaccurate kick for the shooter.

When the researchers at John Moores investigated the psychological dynamics between the kickers and goalies in decades of international matches, they found that moving to the shot within three seconds of the whistle being blown gave the kicker the advantage of surprise. Stalling the kick for more than thirteen seconds had the effect of unnerving the keeper.

The chances of a goal were also increased when kickers waited for the goalie to make the first move, but the success rate dropped by almost half when the kicker waited any longer than 0.41 milliseconds. Longer approaches of just over thirty feet were least successful, while shorter approaches of four to six steps were the most successful.

Professor Tom Riley, one of the researchers involved in the study, concludes that a "well-placed ball, high to the corner, will not be stopped by the goalkeeper even if he anticipates it. There is not enough time to react, so a kick placed in this area would have a 100 percent strike rate." The trick, he concedes, is that the upper corner shot is a more difficult one as opposed to other approaches, such as powering it dead ahead hoping the goalie will move, or going for the inside of the side nettings at a low angle, or the inside of a post.

The fact that the odds are in the kicker's favor does come with a potential drawback: Everyone expects goalies to miss because their job is the more difficult, which means the fear of suffering the shame of having botched what should have been a given can unnerve the kicker. Researchers from the University of Exeter conducted a previous study examining the effects pressure had on a kicker's performance. College players were told to take a series of two penalty kicks while wearing glasses that monitored their eye movements. For their first series they were given no instructions other than to try to score. In the second series, players were informed that the results of their exercise would be made available to the other players, and that the best among them would take home a cash prize. The results showed that a player's tendency to hyperfocus on the keeper positioned in the center of the goal—rather than the goal as a whole—was greater when they experienced heightened anxiety. Since visual and motor control tend to naturally synchronize, anxious players were more likely to kick the ball in the same direction as their focus—and thus essentially kick the ball to the goalie. Lead researcher Greg Wood concludes that the perfect approach for the kicker is to ignore the goalie completely, pick a target, and kick it there.

Not Evolved That Far. Yet.

Cathy Craig and fellow researchers from Queen's University Belfast, Northern Ireland, suggest that a critical reason professional goalies have such a difficult time stopping penalty kicks is due to the limitations of visual system. The human visual system is not sensitive enough for goalies to accurately anticipate the effect that lateral acceleration (spin) will have on the flight path of the ball, and instead predict it to arrive from the direction it was originally sent.

PENMANSHIP

*P*erfect penmanship is much more involved than getting an "A" in your grade-school penmanship class. For the average person, that may be the height of the penmanship achievement. However, those who have reached the pinnacle of perfect penmanship and have received a Master Penman's Certificate from the International Association of Master Penmen, Engrossers and Teachers of Handwriting (IAMPETH) have forgotten a lot more about cursive writing than whatever you may have learned in your elementary school class.

In fact, for the skilled few able to achieve certification, the IAMPETH certificate itself reads: "For superior achievement in the fine art of Penmanship and in keeping the tradition of the great Master Penmen of the past whose skill set the standards by which all future penmen would be judged." Whoa, makes you kind of want one, right? However, there's good reason for the certificate to sound like something out of *Lord of the Rings*; penmanship is an endangered art, thanks to digital technology—although the "golden age" of penmanship is considered to have ended in 1925, after typewriters came into common use.

"The penman and their times are part of our heritage. This, we should remember," Master Penman Michael Sull writes on the IAMPETH website (*www.iampeth.com*) in the "Past Members" section. Each form of penmanship is a specific art, with its own aesthetic, and brings to mind different parts of history for different people. IAMPETH requires a Master Penman to have proficiency in at least two forms, such as Business penmanship, Engrosser's script, Engrossing and Illumination, Offhand Flourishing, Text lettering, and the popular Ornamental and Spencerian script.

Spencerian script is a distinctly American form that brings to mind handwritten letters from the Civil War era, although it was the United States standard until the 1920s, and even has a slight deviation of form for "Spencerian Ladies Hand." The most popular form of script is the Palmer method, which emphasizes use of the arm and shoulder muscles over the finger muscles. And if it's been a while since you've written anything but a quick note by hand, you've probably forgotten what specific and significant muscle development perfect penmanship requires.

But what's the use of perfect penmanship in the digital age? From the Master Penmen of IAMPETH, we can see some gorgeous original art. The art isn't limited to words on paper. Youngest-ever (at twenty-seven) Master Penman and artist Jake Weidmann uses his penmanship skills to create pieces depicting a skull made up of script and poetry, a finely lined phoenix-like bird, and a clipper ship in a sea of words, all chic enough to make the steampunk-iest hipster covet them—for a tattoo, no doubt.

Perfect . . .

PERFUME

*B*lack-and-white commercials depicting women in bikinis rolling around on the beach. Men with open shirts racing expensive cars. Depictions of models whispering words like "obsession," "desire," and "lust." Typical perfume ad, right?

But for all those advertising dollars, the perfect perfume has actually been described by MSNBC as "Eau de DNA"—and it's exactly what it sounds like: smell preference governed by genetics. You see, not only do genetics determine what smells you enjoy on others; they also determine which are the best for you to wear.

The nose is a fairly complicated organ, with about 400 subtypes of smell receptors, and scientists are just beginning to understand the organization and scales regarding reception of scent information. Compare this with the structure of the eyes or the ear, which have been clearly understood and even fairly easily taught. No one can easily explain the nose, but scientists already knew that sexual attraction to someone's scent was controlled by major histocompatibility complex genes, known as MHC. Humans are attracted to others with MHC different from their own, which biologists theorize is to keep us from mating with anyone who might be a relation. Now new evidence has linked MHC with influencing scent preferences that have nothing to do with avoiding inbreeding, but rather with normal perfume-range scents like vanilla, cedar, and rose.

In a study published December 6, 2011, in the *International Journal of Cosmetic Science*, August Hammerli—who has been doing scent-related research for years with the Swiss Federal Institute of Technology in Zürich—was able to sniff out a few details about what makes a certain smell perfect for you. When Hammerli's test subjects inhaled a variety of scents there were clear winners and losers, such as the vanilla-like tolu, from a South American tree, which consistently rated high, and vetiver, an earthy scent from Indian grass, which ranked lowest. Hammerli noticed a strong correlation between scent preferences and the subject's MHC genes.

According to Professor Tim Jacob, a smell and taste specialist with Cardiff University, "There is a statistical correlation that shows there is a link between our immunotype and our fragrance preference. It seems that you choose the perfume that reflects your immune system." Theoretically, by "wearing" our immune system as a fragrance, we can attract a partner with a different immune system in order to create the most diverse immune system for our offspring.

Perfect odor matching to find your perfume may be extremely science based in the future. Hammerli's company, Basisnote, has been negotiating with online dating sites to work scent into dating profiles using a simple saliva test to determine your MHC and matching you with a code that describes it. Not only a date, but your truly, genetically, individually perfect perfume could be just a spritz away!

POPULARLY PERFECT

The bestselling perfume of all time is Chanel No. 5, which has been on top since its launch in 1921. Marilyn Monroe was famously photographed for the perfume, and was noted to have provocatively said the perfume was the only thing she wore to bed.

Perfect . . .

PHOTOGRAPH

*D*escribing what makes art perfect has confounded philosophers for ages, but based on technical merit, social impact, and aesthetics, we can turn to photography textbooks, see what is taught, and analyze whether photographs that we see make the grade.

An example of a perfect photograph is "Afghan Girl" by Steve McCurry, which exceeds in every category any professor could present. The 1984 photo of Sharbat Gula in a refugee camp became the June 1985 cover of *National Geographic* and is one of the most recognizable photographs in the world. National Public Radio described it as "one of the century's most iconic" photographs, with widely circulated publications including *Time* magazine and *USA Today* echoing the sentiments. Interestingly enough, the photo editor at *National Geographic* initially dismissed the photograph as "too disturbing" for the cover, but McCurry pushed it through to the editor in chief, who actually jumped out of his seat when he saw it.

The technical merits of the photograph are immediately apparent on viewing it. The lighting is perfectly luminous, without shadow, and precisely accentuates the colors. The main two colors are blue and red, opposites on the color wheel, and thus create a striking contrast.

Henri Cartier-Besson who is known as the "father of photojournalism," has said, "In photography, visual organization can only stem from a developed instinct." In an interview with The Chautauqua Institution in 2010, McCurry's account of capturing the shot gives the viewer an insight into his process and instincts:

"She was trying to be modest . . . , she had her hands up to her face, but the light was still not quite right, and that kind of connection still wasn't as strong as I wanted it to be," McCurry said. "Then, the teacher kind of coached her to relax. She said, this really is important for us to get the story out about this refugee situation, we want the world to know . . . so she (the girl) dropped her hands, and the light was right, and the background . . . and she just looked directly into my lens. And for literally just two exposures, I got this very concentrated, very intense look on her face. And then it was gone."

The photograph was taken on Kodachrome film, and was so successful that Kodak gave McCurry the very last roll of Kodachrome ever produced. *Associated Press* writer Ben Dobbin described "Afghan Girl" as "one of the finest illustrations of the film's (Kodachrome) subtle rendering of light, contrast, and color harmony."

Photography students have been required to study the colors, the lines, the circles of the eyes, the face, the clothing, but the majority of viewers were fascinated by the subject's haunting green-eyed gaze. The public interest was so great that McCurry and *National Geographic* made several attempts to find Gula, but were not successful until 2002, when she was approximately age thirty—she was not aware of her exact age, as she was orphaned young during the Soviet bombing of Pakistan. Biometric technology had to be used to match her unique iris pattern to concretely identify her, as over the years many imposters came forward claiming to be her. Indeed, McCurry happily shared the profits with his subject once he located her, ensuring better lives for Gula's children.

National Geographic set up the "Afghan Girls Fund," which later became the "Afghan Children's Fund." The photograph has been listed by various sources as one of the photographs that "changed the world."

PERSONS UNKNOWN

When Steve McCurry located Sharbat Gula in 2002, she was a devout Muslim living a remote life in Afghanistan with her three daughters and her husband. Although she remembered having the photograph taken, "I don't think she was particularly interested in her fame," McCurry said. "But she was pleased when we said she had come to be a symbol of the dignity and resilience of her people."

PITCH

*P*erfect pitch—also called absolute pitch—is the ability to identify tones without any accompanying context. When a note is played on a piano, a person with perfect pitch can name the note. Some are even able to hear a chord and identify the individual notes. When a garbage truck makes a slow, agonizing screech as it comes to a stop at the end of your block, a person with perfect pitch would not only be annoyed, but would also be able to tell you in which key it screeched.

It's also possible to have perfect pitch if you can't read music. For example, a musician from a remote location who doesn't use written music might still have perfect pitch, and could demonstrate by replicating notes on an instrument. Some people simply can't read sheet music but can still identify and copy a note. This is sometimes seen in people with autism; a study from Laurent Mottron and J. Burack in 2001 found "pitch processing is advanced in 'high-functioning' autism."

PEOPLE ENDOWED WITH PERFECT PITCH:
- Leonard Bernstein
- Ritchie Blackmore
- Michelle Branch

- Mariah Carey
- Nat "King" Cole
- Bing Crosby
- Mia Farrow
- Jimi Hendrix
- Phil Lesh
- Paul Shaffer
- Barbra Streisand
- Stevie Wonder

Oddly enough, one doesn't need perfect pitch to be a great musician, nor does perfect pitch guarantee musical skill. People who speak tonal languages such as Mandarin and other Sino-Tibetan languages have a unique form of perfect pitch. While not all Asian languages are tonal, there's some evidence that a predisposition to perfect pitch is related to Asian genetics. A study by the Eastman Music School in Rochester, New York, found that a surprising 63 percent of its Asian students had perfect pitch, compared to the 7 percent of non-Asian students who did.

Some say that people are born with perfect pitch, but there's also research suggesting that it can be developed as an infant. However, if you're reading this and don't have it now, you're pretty much out of luck. What can be learned, however, is relative pitch. With relative pitch, a person memorizes a tone (all of us can develop tonal memory), and can then identify pitch in relation to that. It's not perfect, but, for most of us, it'll have to do.

NOT AMUSIA'ING

Amusia may be considered the opposite of perfect pitch. It's the physical inability to process pitch—the inability to distinguish one note from another, different one—and is both inborn and acquired, although only 4 percent of the population has the congenital form. Amusia is not to be confused with tone deafness, which is how people generally refer to the inability to distinguish musical notes. The true existence of tone "deafness" is debatable, because unlike amusia, it can be eliminated with training.

Perfect . . .

PLACE TO TAKE A NAP

*T*he perfect place to nap is in a hammock. There's an instinctive motivation in all of us to be soothed by gentle rocking. Whether that's because it takes us back to the womb, or because as babies we were cradled and rocked to sleep more often than not, it still holds true.

But do hammocks actually put you to sleep? Yes. Researchers at the Sleep and Cognition Neuroimaging Lab at the University of Geneva in Switzerland tested it out. Their "hammock" for the study was a specially made bed that swayed gently from side to side. The test subjects spent time sleeping in the "hammock" and in conventional beds. The "hammock" led to a faster transition to sleep in each participant. Additionally, given the environment in which the study took place, the benefits of the rocking were not just attributable to being in a real hammock by a lake at a cabin in the woods or somewhere scenic.

When sleeping in the hammock, subjects had a longer period of N2 sleep, a type of non–rapid eye movement sleep that generally accounts for half of the time you spend asleep at night. Subjects also showed a dramatic increase in brain-wave patterns in the "hammock" during deep sleep. The researchers had expected the swaying to put people out faster, but were surprised to see the improved quality of sleep people experienced while in the hammock. "Motion has a specific effect on the brain," said Sophie Schwartz, a neuroscientist with the study. "Not only does rocking make us fall asleep more quickly, but it also makes people sleep more deeply."

Coauthor of the study Dr. Michael Muhlethaler first became interested in motion and sleep when he observed the frequency with which train passengers would fall asleep. In a 2011 interview with National Public Radio, Muhlethaler said of the rocking, "It's not that it brings new (brain) waves. It just fortifies waves that are naturally there, intrinsically."

It is notable that this initial study involved only men, as the menstrual cycle of women can affect sleep and the brain's electrical activity. Schwartz is confident that women will experience the same benefits, and studies are now under way to include both genders and full nights of sleep.

ROCKING HORSE

In the thirteenth century, people reported seeing Mongol warriors sleeping while riding their horses. While Mongols were trained to ride at age three and were notoriously hard-riding, they may also have been able to tap into the benefits of the rocking motion for sleep.

Perfect . . .

POEM

There are countless lovely and moving poems in the world, but it's Emily Dickinson's "The Chariot" (also known as "712") that was praised as "perfect" and "flawless" by critic Allen Tate in his 1939 book *Reactionary Essays on Poems and Ideas*. "The framework of the poem," Tate writes, "is, in fact, the two abstractions, mortality and eternity . . . in perfect equality with the images: she sees the ideas, and thinks the perceptions."

The famous first two lines of the poem read: "Because I could not stop for Death, / He kindly stopped for me." On its surface, the poem is merely the tale of a carriage ride with Death and Immortality. But, upon further analysis, there are many debatable meanings. Some think the poem was intended to be a metaphor for a funeral, a rumination on life, or even a celebration of the eternal soul.

In *Emily Dickinson's Poetry: Stairway of Surprise* (1960) critic Charles R. Anderson writes, "The poem is flawless to the last detail, each image precise and discrete." He pinpoints how Dickinson utilizes a variety of literary devices to best communicate a host of emotions, physical descriptions, and character, as well as wrap humanity and art's greatest themes—life, love, death, and immortality—in a cloak of thought-provoking mystery. The structure of the poem is strong and precisely structured. It is composed of six quatrains (sections that are four lines each) that feature internal rhyme throughout and that each terminate in end rhyme, close rhyme, or visual rhyme.

The meter of the internal lines alternates between iambic tetrameter (four metric feet that create eight syllables per line) and iambic trimeter (three metric feet that result in six syllables per line). In case you're not well versed in poetic-speak, iambic trimeter and tetrameter rotate unstressed and stressed syllables—da DA da DA da DA da DA. This structure of iambic trimeter and tetrameter is actually the same structure as the *Gilligan's Island* catchy theme song. In fact, the whole beautiful, classic, and highly studied poem "The Chariot" can be perfectly sung to its melody.

Just try to resist doing that in public.

Perfect . . .

POUR OF GUINNESS

The Irish are picky about their beer and even pickier about their Guinness. Diageo, the company that owns the Guinness brand, is very specific about how to pour a Guinness. In fact, there's a "perfect pint" class available at the Guinness factory in Dublin, Ireland.

The "perfect pour" is a double pour from the tap into what should be a "tulip-shaped pint glass." The first pour itself should take exactly 119.53 seconds. The glass should be held at a 45-degree angle, with the beer poured straight down the inside side of the glass, which is tipped away from you, toward the tap. As the beer flows to the tap, it is first passed through a "chiller," and at the end of the tap it's pushed through a "restrictor" plate perforated with five holes. This increases both friction and pressure, resulting in the bubbles that create a rich head. In a perfect pour, the perfect head is created, as pouring all at once will create too much head and a slightly more bitter flavor. Too much carbonation can be tasted, as CO_2 is detected by sour-detecting taste buds. The side pour also helps enable the perfect amount of carbonation. As the glass fills, tilt it back up, and stop when it's two-thirds full. That's the end of the first pour. Now the glass should be left to sit until settled, which takes approximately a minute and a half. Top off with a slow second pour, ending with the head forming a gentle convex shape at the top of the glass. Using the last small stream, draw a shamrock in the foam. Draught Guinness should be served at 42.8°F. If the Guinness is in a can, Diageo would like you to pour it—"in one smooth action"—into a large glass.

The perfect pour is a specifically modern aesthetic, as only a few decades ago, Irish drinkers preferred their beer warmer, and Guinness took four minutes to pour simply sitting under the tap, without the glass being handled by the bartender. At a lower temp, the beer was foamier, hence the slower pour.

MORE LIKE AN APPETIZER

Is the Guinness available in the United States the same as the fabled beer in Ireland? No. The Guinness served in the States comes from regional breweries subcontracted by Guinness. And despite endless references to it being a "meal in a glass," it's actually one of the lighter beers on the market, the result of light ale mixed with Guinness Flavor Extract, or GFE—a dark, sticky, and smoke-flavored additive.

Perfect . . .

PUNCH (BOXING)

*T*here are a lot of different ways to punch someone: Uppercut, cross, jab, twist punch . . . the list goes on and on. But according to writer Martin Kane, as published in the May 13, 1957, issue of *Sports Illustrated*, "The perfect punch is always a left hook . . . against a strong-jawed man who has not been weakened by a long, hard fight. It comes fast and it executes instantly."

In 1957, boxing legend Sugar Ray Robinson threw the punch that inspired Kane's description.

Robinson had won the middleweight championship in 1951, only to lose it six years later to Gene Fullmer. During their rematch in May of 1957, Robinson patiently waited to exploit an aspect of Fullmer he had noticed in the first fight—Fullmer was sometimes open to a left hook. In the fifth round, seemingly out of nowhere, Robinson delivered a right to the body that resulted in Fullmer's head moving to the left, and as Fullmer went to compensate and swing back with his right, Robinson was ready. Robinson struck with such precise timing that Kane's *SI* article revealed that the spectators were in agreement that Fullmer "walked" into Robinson's left hook, and "[f]or a while thereafter he couldn't walk at all." It was the first time in his forty-four-fight career that Fullmer had been knocked out. He was hit hard enough that when he teetered back to his corner after the count, he asked his coach why the fight had been stopped, and even hours later still had no recollection of what had happened. Of that punch, Kane observed that in "all the history of boxing, the perfect punch never has been so well delivered," and "with so much at stake."

The punch served its purpose without gruesome damage. It was strong enough to silence the nearly 15,000 fans watching live, strong enough to knock out Fullmer and make history, and yet, almost miraculously, Fullmer wasn't bruised or swollen. Even famous boxing trainer Emanuel Stewerd and Fullmer's own trainer Marv Jensen both described Robinson's hit as "the perfect punch," and boxing critics agreed.

Robinson was inducted into the International Boxing Hall of Fame in 1990, and in 1997 the boxing magazine *The Ring* named him the best pound-for-pound boxer of all time. Joe Lewis, Sugar Ray Leonard, and even Muhammad Ali—who never missed an opportunity to refer to himself as "The Greatest"—considered Robinson, the man who delivered the perfect punch, to be the greatest boxer of all time.

Perfect . . .

ROCK-SKIPPING ANGLE

*S*kipping rocks is a childhood pastime that you may remember with a sense of nostalgia. But perhaps you also remember how hard it can be to get the damn rock to actually skip in the first place! Turns out that getting it right is all about the angle.

According to physicist Lyderic Bocquet, the perfect rock-skipping angle is 20 degrees. If the rock hits the water at a 20-degree angle, he says, "The stone still has more chances to re-bounce than for any other angle." Bocquet would know. A physics professor at Claude Bernard Lyon University, Bocquet was intrigued when his son asked him why the rocks they tossed skipped, instead of sinking. Fellow physicist Christophe Clanet became interested in the project as well, and suggested they investigate it together . . . by first building a robot: a rock-skipping robot that could send metal discs across water with absolute precision. Sure, why not?

Their first big discovery—which seems to pale in comparison to building a robot to do your bidding—was that the magic angle was 20 degrees, at which the discs always skipped further. That proved true regardless of whether some of the initial conditions, such as velocity or rotation, were changed as the robot released the discs. As long as they maintained the 20-degree angle, the discs *always* had more opportunities to skip farther than at any other angle. In their paper,

"Secrets of successful stone-skipping," which was published in a 2004 issue of *Nature,* they concluded that the success behind that angle was that it allowed for only the briefest impact between the disc and water, resulting in a minimum amount of drag.

Bocquet explains a stone will skip on the water in the same way a person water-skiing will skim the water's surface. Both the skier and the stone experience force from the water, in relation to the velocity with which either moves across it. As their speed increases, so does their lift. As the boat stops, the water-skier sinks. For the stone, the spin is needed to stabilize the stone as it skips off the water and travels through the air, and give it angular momentum. That spin is seen in expert throwers as a flick of the wrist.

Confident that they'd cracked the code, Bocquet and Clanet set out to break what was then the world record, which had been set in 2002 by Kurt Steiner when he sent a stone forty skips. They set the robot to pitch faster, but instead of breaking the world record the machine developed a bad case of vibration, and vibrated out of control while dropping parts. Typical over-excitable 'bot. In addition, despite his newfound depth of understanding of skipping rocks, Bocquet still struggles to make the successful leap from theory to practice—having peaked at fifteen skips, the exact inverse of the current record of fifty-one skips held by Russ Byars.

WHO LET THE FROGS OUT?

"Skipping rocks" is not the only term for skipping rocks. In the UK, you'd hear it called "ducks and drakes." In both Sweden and Finland, pick up a stone and fire it across the water and you're "throwing a sandwich." In the Ukraine, kids picking up flat stones by the water might be planning to "let the frogs out," or in Poland about to "let the ducks out," while in Spain they'll be busy "making white caps." But no matter what you call it, the perfect angle is 20 degrees.

SALARY

*E*veryone dreams of becoming a millionaire. You'd go on elaborate vacations. You'd lie around all day next to your salt-water pool. You'd collect antique cars, ancient swords, or more stamps than you can count to fill your idle hours. You'd think that tons of money would make you the happiest person that you could be . . . but that's just not true. In fact, the perfect salary is just $75,000 a year for an individual. Not exactly Warren Buffett territory, but our old friend science is at hand to tell us that money can only buy a finite amount of happiness.

Nobel prize winner Daniel Kahneman and economist Angus Deaton analyzed 450,000 responses to Gallup and Healthways polls in a 2010 Princeton University study, and revealed that both emotional well-being and life evaluation increased as a person's salary increased, yet emotional well-being peaked at $75,000 and was no different at higher salaries. "Having money clearly takes the sting out of adversities," reported Belinda Luscombe in the September 6, 2010, issue of *Time* magazine. $75,000 was just the magic number at which people seemed to relax about having enough to spare. "It does seem to me a plausible number at which people would think money was not an issue," Deaton commented.

Two forms of happiness were studied: day-to-day mood and the deeper satisfaction with life. Life satisfaction seemed to level off at $75,000, with day-to-day mood having capacity to improve or decline, as day-to-day moods do. As the Kahneman and Deaton study sums up, "High incomes don't bring you happiness, but they do bring you a life you think is better." However, it failed to find why these feelings leveled off at $75,000. If only Christopher Wallace, aka Notorious B.I.G., were still alive, maybe he could help researchers take a more definitive look at his hypothesis: "Mo' money, mo' problems."

CAN'T BUY ME LOVE?

In the book *The Science of Love: Rational Answers to the Irrational Emotions of Adoring, Caring, Longing, and Heartbreak*, author and scientist Uldis Sprogis points out that while the old saying is true—love cannot be bought—caring behaviors can be. For example, a caregiver in a hospital is paid but also may love being nurturing and love the work, and thus love the people involved. Now that's perfection!

SANDCASTLE

*Y*ou're at the beach and you set out to build the perfect sand-castle. Instead, you spend two hours packing sand into a bucket and end up with something only kinda, sorta impressive before the tide comes in and washes it all away. The good news is that according to reports from *BBC Focus TV*, *The Guardian*, and *The Telegraph*, all of which have put scientists to work on the quest, the perfect sandcastle isn't all that hard to create.

According to *BBC Focus TV*, the perfect weather for building a sandcastle is slightly overcast and cool, so that the moisture used doesn't evaporate, and the "foundation stays firmer and more solid." They advised beachgoers to build just above the high tide line, where one can easily dig down to wet sand, and high enough to avoid the tide when it rolls back in.

Andy Ridgway with *BBC Focus TV* tested the popular theory of using eight parts sand to one part water and found that the exact ratio worked well—but so did using less water. "It's not too critical, the level of water," Ridgway said. "The water binds the grains of sand together . . . but if you increase the level of water, the surface tension in the water decreases. But at the same time, the width of the bridges in the water increases, so those two factors counteract each other." Bridges are formed by water molecules connecting grains of sand.

In Lucinda Wierenga's *Sandcastles Made Simple*, she advises that, with all that water, you shouldn't forget about drainage: "Successful sand sculptors do not use plastic buckets or other closed moulds but build their shapes by stacking handfuls of wet sand or tamping it down in a topless and bottomless form."

Ian Taylor with *BBC Focus TV* recommends using a spray bottle to keep the castle moist once you start building. "Once you have your overall shape ready, you can get your tools . . . and you can start to be a little more accurate . . . and it's these little tools that are going to provide the finishing touches."

Even the grains of sand themselves are relevant, says J. V. Chamary with *BBC Focus TV*. The perfect shape for building is an angular grain, to create friction and stick best. Using a sieve, you can sift through for the finest grains, which pack together best. The scientists with *The Telegraph* agree heartily, emphasizing the importance of fine particles.

And, for those all-important finishing touches, Wierenga reminds the builder to not use too much pressure at the top of the structure, and to "carve conservatively. Once sand has been carved away, there is no easy way to put it back."

It may seem like some people take their sandcastles a little too seriously, but videos of competitions reveal that an appropriately fun attitude prevails. The annual U.S. Open Sandcastle Competition offers $21,000 in cash prizes, and can be a perfect way for an artist to show the community what he or she can create.

Perfect . . .

SANDWICH

While you're powering through a spin class or nursing a hangover, the perfect sandwich might just be your best friend, but you don't have to make do with a second-rate sub. For advice on how to make a perfect sandwich, follow this expert guidance from our sandwich advisors: There's chef advice from Bobby Flay from *People* Magazine of May 4, 2011; nutrition advice from dietitian Dalhia Campbell; guru advice from Sisha Ortuzar, cofounder of 'wichcraft gourmet sandwich shop of New York City; and scientific advice from Hervé This and Daniel Bennett, from *BBC Focus* magazine. So ready your mind and masticators. (Ahem! That means chewing teeth.)

The Bread

Hervé This recommends a bread like a baguette—crunchy on the outside and soft on the inside, because "our brain is designed to recognize contrast." In the same way that people stop noticing a smell commonly around them, we may become fatigued of a homogeneous texture in a recipe. Ortuzar agrees, and told *Men's Health* readers to skip the toaster and just brown one side on a skillet, placing the toasted sides inward so there's a barrier to prevent sogginess, and mouths aren't scratched by the toasted part. Ortuzar also advises that if you like a lot of heavy, wet ingredients, slice a thick piece of bread for the bottom.

The Condiments

Bobby Flay recommends slathering mayonnaise on *both* sides of the bread, because "it's going to double the amount of moisture you're going to get in the sandwich, and of course, the flavor." (The outer mayo will be absorbed in the later step—pan crisping.) Hervé This and Daniel Bennett recommend a thin layer of butter on the bread to create a "hydrophobic barrier" to keep the bread from sucking up sauce moisture and to "carry the flavor compounds via your saliva to your papillae—the taste centers of your mouth."

Guts and Glory

The inner ingredients of the perfect sandwich vary by taste and dietary restrictions. Ortuzar recommends placing cheese next to the bread, then the meat for optimal flavor, along with lightly seasoned greens. Flay's "perfect sandwich" uses turkey instead of other fattier meats—stacked with cheese, coleslaw, and greens with Thousand Island dressing. Campbell told *The Sun*, "The combination of the slow-release carbohydrates in the bread and the protein and calcium in the cheese will keep your blood sugar more stable so you'll feel less tired and irritable." Campbell recommends avocado for a vitamin E boost, sardines for omega-3 fatty acids if you need help concentrating, or peanut butter and banana to fuel a workout. Bacon is another enhancer, not just via its flavor but also from its texture, according to Dr. Graham Clayton from the Department of Food Science at Leeds University. If you don't eat pork, try turkey bacon, and if you don't eat meat, try a smoky tempeh bacon made of soybeans.

Veg Out

Still not convinced that veggies are a key ingredient? Hervé This explains, "The more you chew on in each bite, the more flavor you get with each mouthful, the less you need to eat to feel satisfied." "Bright, colorful fruits and vegetables such as beetroot," says Campbell, "are packed with antioxidants to keep your immune system fully charged."

Finishing Touches

Both Flay and Hervé This think finishing with heat is key. Flay's choice is to crisp in a pan. Hervé This and Bennett explain the science behind it: "Heat excites essential oils in the ingredients, carrying most of the flavor into the air, meaning you'll taste more via your nasal canals."

While the invention of the sandwich is attributed to John Montagu, the Earl of Sandwich, in the 1760s, evidence of sandwich consumption dates back to ancient Jewish history as well as the Middle Ages. Surely with its illustrious past, the sandwich also has a bright future, so keep experimenting to find your personal perfect, and *bon appetit.*

SCRABBLE SCORE

Scrabble exists in many different forms—especially as various online games—but the original, official Scrabble is a board game made by Hasbro. It was originally conceived in 1938 by the unfortunately named American architect Alfred Mosher Butts, and passed hands through various people and manufacturers before ending up with Hasbro and enjoying its current popularity. With Scrabble tournaments being played worldwide, a perfect Scrabble game is a real though lofty goal. The perfect game of Scrabble would be one in which a player scored with a few of the "perfect" Scrabble words, which would result in scores as yet unheard of. Most of the theoretically highest-scoring words are theoretical because no one (recorded, in tournament) has been able to play them.

SCRABBLE PERFECTS

- The highest possible score one can make on the first move will use all your letters, will spell "MUZJIKS," which is the word for "peasants" in Russian, and give you 128 points.
- Though it has never happened in a regulation game, the chemical "BENZOXYCAMPHORS" played across the edges of the board would net you 1,970 points, and maybe your fifteen minutes of fame.

- Benjamin Woo of Vancouver, British Columbia, scored a single-word record by playing "OXYPHENBUTAZONE" for 1,458 points—in a "theoretical" and not officially recognized game.
- In a competition game, Karl Khoshnaw of Manchester, England, played "CAZIQUES," the plural for "West Indian Chief," and received 392 points.
- In 1989, Philip Appleby from Lymington, England, set the record for the highest score ever achieved in one game with 1,049 points.
- Nathan Hedt of North Adelaide, South Australia, scored 3,986 points in a theoretical game of Scrabble. Since it was not an actual game, Appleby still holds the record, but Hedt's efforts give Scrabble lovers a goal to reach toward.

Wonder how many points "perfect" would net?

SEXUAL POSITION

There are sixty-four sexual positions detailed in the *Kama Sutra*, ranging in difficulty from easy to "you'd have to be an acrobat." But of all these different options, the perfect sexual position is the overwhelmingly popular missionary position, which owes its high ranking to a bit of biology. The missionary position is the term for the sexual position where the man is on top, but that's about as far as the definition goes. The *Kama Sutra* and the Chinese *Pillow Book* describe many variations of this position, all of which fall under the man-on-top description and thus would still be considered "missionary." It's only a myth that the name of the position came from Christian missionaries, but its etymology is debatable—not much is recorded about its usage before Alfred Kinsey's 1948 *Sexual Behavior in the Human Male*.

Missionary position was the number one position as reported in *The New Book of Lists* by David Wallechinsky and Amy Wallace, due to the face-to-face intimacy and the fact that compared to other positions, it doesn't require anyone to be particularly athletic. Author of *The Sex Book*, Suzy Godsend, described a study in the Netherlands in which missionary position was studied under magnetic resonance imaging (MRI) and described: "The images illustrate the very natural fit of the male and female genitals in position."

Playboy and *Men's Health* have both advised using a pillow under the woman's hips to maximize clitoral stimulation while in the missionary position. The pillow trick is also advised for couples trying to get pregnant, which means missionary might be either perfect or the absolutely worst thing ever depending on how you feel about being a parent nine months after taking the sexy-pillow advice.

Askmen.com, in an article by Isabella Snow, renamed the position "The Comfort Zone," and admonished critics that the position is only boring if "you're lacking passion and creativity." Besides the freedom that lovers' hands have in this position, Snow reminds readers of the mouth-to-ear proximity for, ahem, communication.

On Nerve.com, Rebecca Archer's *In Praise of the Missionary Position* says, "If she lines up just right, his pelvic bone presses her magic button better than any reach-around, and if she puts her hips into it, she can thrust with as much gusto as he does. It's the most skin-to-skin contact for your money."

In 1988, psychotherapist Edward Eichel formulated what is called the "coital alignment technique" (CAT), which was published in the *Journal of Sex & Marital Therapy*. In CAT, the male lies above the female, but instead of being chest to chest with his penis moving mostly horizontally, the man moves forward toward the female's shoulders so the base of the penis stimulates the woman's clitoris. Instead of thrusting, the couple rocks, with the woman pushing up and the man pressing down. Eichel points out that this also stimulates both the urethral meatus on the woman, which is a densely nerved area below the G-spot, and the prostatic nerves for the man. CAT has been repeatedly scientifically proven to result in, as *Psychology Today* put it, "easier orgasms for women."

As evidenced by the *Kama Sutra*, finding a perfect variation on the missionary position is nothing new, and even Eichel admits of CAT, "Many couples have discovered this spontaneously."

Unlucky Irish

In 2011's *Psychology: Concepts and Connections (10th edition)*, Spencer A. Rathus writes about the small island off the coast of Ireland called Inis Beag, where "premarital sex is all but unknown." The inhabitants only have missionary-position sex, in the dark, with their clothes on, and only for the sake of producing children. A woman who might (accidentally) enjoy sex is considered "deviant," and men are expected to finish up with the disgusting task of sex as quickly as possible.

Perfect . . .

SHAVE (FACE)

The perfect shave is an art—which is something that barbers have known for many years. But as technology moves forward, shaving tech isn't quite as popular as gaming systems and smartphones, and the quality of most men's shaves has actually degraded with time. But to get the perfect shave you don't have to live next to a barbershop; you only have to follow some basic rules from Gillette's Technology Centre in Reading, England.

Be Prepared

Hair shaves best after a hot shower; if that's not possible, wash your face with hot water. The heat removes the sebum (the oily substance produced by sebaceous glands) and allows the water to penetrate the hair, softening it. Water at 119°F will kill most of the bacteria that cause post-shave irritation. (The U.S. Consumer Product Safety Commission warns that more than five minutes of exposure to 120°F water *may* cause third-degree burns, so don't nap in it.)

Check Your Tools

You need just two basic tools for a perfect shave:

- **The razor.** Multiblade razors may seem like hype—and maybe they are—but their popularity apparently isn't due to hype alone, as research has proven over two-thirds of men prefer multiblade razors, with the four- and five-blade versions triumphing over the three-blades. A practical reason for this is that, depending on the stroke, between 1.1 to 300 pounds of force are exerted onto the skin via the razor, and the greater surface area of the razor spreads out the force. The layers of razor also serve to lift the hair; as one blade lifts, another blade slices the hair, for a closer shave.
- **The brush.** A shaving brush serves several purposes; it exfoliates the skin, delivers a richer lather than fingers can, and helps lift hair and keep it suspended in lather, ripe for the razor swipe. Badger-hair brushes are very popular, but technology has brought some amazing synthetic brushes that are more hygienic than the bacteria-prone and porous animal hair. Check out award-winning synthetic brushes like the men-u Premier, and the Pure Performance from Jack Black.

Lube Up

Look for shaving cream or gel with an oil base to form a protective layer between the skin and the razor. Aloe vera has positively charged molecules that may balance the negatively charged skin, but has yet to be proven. Gillette Fusion ProGuide Shave Gel won the 2011 *FHM* magazine "Men's Grooming Award." If you want to go fancier, try *Esquire's* 2011 "Grooming Award" pick, Kyoku for Men Sake Infused shave cream, which also got a shout-out from *GQ*.

Get Down to Business

Take your first pass shaving with the grain, to avoid razor burn. After that first pass, you've weeded it down enough to go against the grain, which is a closer but potentially more irritating shave method.

Seal It Up

Splash the face with cold water to close your pores. Gently pat dry with a clean, soft, natural-fiber towel. Apply a moisturizer made specifically for post-shave. *GQ* recommends Bleu De Chanel Aftershave Balm by Chanel. About.com's readers voted for The Bluebeard's Revenge Post Shave Balm, which at the very least looks pretty cool on your bathroom shelf.

If you are—or know—a guy who has been thinking of bearding up to hide minor facial flaws like scars and bumps, remember that *The Daily Mail*'s February 19, 2010, issue published a study in which an overwhelming 91 percent of women surveyed on men's appearance preferred "a guy who had a few flaws over one who is perfect."

Perfect . . .

SKIING POWDER

*I*f you're a skier or snowboarder you already know that the perfect skiing powder is a soft and smooth blanket of fine-grain flakes. Packed in thick layers, it is generally a more forgiving surface to hit at high speeds than crud, crust, or slush. But the next time someone tells you they "just skied *the best* powder," if you want to be obstinate, you can point out that in fact, he did not.

The reason for that is because the best powder is orbiting Saturn. Paul Schenk of the Lunar and Planetary Institute in Houston, Texas, says Enceladus, the sixth-largest moon of Saturn, has been slowly developing a powder base as deep as 325 feet in some places, for the last they're-not-entirely-sure-how-many millions of years. Yes, millions. And it's some seriously sweet powder, too. Somewhat similar to what you might see on a good day at Yellowstone but far superior, produced by geysers spewing a finer ice particle than skiers on Earth have yet to experience. The surface also boasts vast, powder-filled canyons and craters. Dr. Schenk described the ice particles as "even finer than talcum powder" and adds, "This would make for the finest powder a skier could hope for."

The downsides of this skiing paradise are the roughly 750-million-mile (one way!) trip, skiing while wearing a large space suit and breathing equipment, and dealing with gravity just one-hundredth that of Earth, in which you might come in at under two pounds, making your average Chihuahua seem heavy in comparison.

SMILE

In the mid-nineteenth century, French physician Guillaume Duchenne identified two very distinct types of smiles while studying the physiology of facial expressions. His approach was to pass electrical currents through subjects' facial muscles and take pictures of what they looked like throughout. In the smile that came to bear his name, he found that the zygomatic major muscle contracted to raise the corner of the lips, and at the same time the orbicularis oculi muscles around the eyes contracted. This brought about the perfect smile, the type of smile people associate with genuine joy.

In the other type of smile, only the zygomaticus muscles contract, which people generally felt represented a "fake" smile. The absence of the orbicularis oculi's contraction is most obviously seen when "crow's feet" smile lines at the eye fail to appear, a contraction that is involuntary and cannot be faked.

More recent science has been able to examine the brain function involved in smiling. It's fairly logical that the motor cortex controls a fake smile, just as it controls the other voluntary facial motions. A genuine Duchenne smile comes from the emotional center of the brain, called the limbic system, specifically the cingulate cortex. Dr. Martin Seligman calls the fake smile the "Pan American Smile," after the polite and duty-bound smiles of the Pan Am airline flight attendants often featured in the company's advertising.

In a 2001 issue of *Developmental Psychology*, the Duchenne smile was called "the most positive expression of happiness the face can convey." A University of California–Berkeley study found that women expressing the Duchenne smile were happier with their lives and more likely to be married. A similar Australian study in 2006 found that those displaying a "Pan American" smile were less happy with their lives overall. So next time you see a hint of "crow's feet" in the mirror, just remember it's actually a sign of perfection.

POINTY, PEARLY WHITES

Cosmetic dental work is on the rise in the United States, with people dropping thousands for the white, even teeth that enhance a smile. But in Japan, the current trend is for crooked teeth and pointy, "snaggle" canines. The look is called "Yaeba," meaning "double tooth," and is thought to make one look younger, as the condition occurs naturally in growing teens. It also makes a beautiful woman seem more approachable, with a "cute" flaw.

Perfect . . .

SOUP

*S*plit pea. Veggie. Corn chowder. There are so many soups to choose from that it may seem difficult to pick the one that's perfect. However, there is one soup that's not just delicious, but has amazing health benefits, too.

Have you already guessed? Yes—it's chicken soup. If you look back to examine the cuisine of ancient civilizations, you'll discover that nearly every culture has developed a version of this truly classic soup. That's probably because it not only tastes good, it's good for you, too.

The first noted association connecting chicken soup with its ability to fight the common cold was during the time of the Roman emperor Nero (68–36 B.C.). Around 60 B.C., physician Pedacius Dioscorides recommended the emperor try it to alleviate his respiratory discomfort. It was also a favorite go-to for twelfth-century rabbi and medical expert Moses Maimonides, who served it to the military leader Sultan Saladin when the officer had a cold. Maimonides also recommended the dish for hemorrhoids, constipation, and leprosy in addition to colds and flu. Later on, the dish became such an important food within the Jewish community—especially for the Ashkenazi of Central and Eastern Europe, who also serve it on Shabbat and special occasions—that it became nicknamed "Jewish penicillin."

Finally, in 1978, scientists found some truth behind the long-held belief in the curative properties of this well-known soup. The medical journal *Chest* published the scientists'discovery that chicken soup was more effective than hot water in increasing the movement of nasal mucus within the chest cavity and that it also helps prevent colds by strengthening the protective cilia in the nose. Then, in 2000, Dr. Stephen Rennard published a follow-up study in *Chest*. In his article "Chicken Soup Inhibits Neutrophil Chemotaxis *In Vitro*," he outlined the benefits of chicken soup, among them reducing the inflammatory response that causes congestion and helping to hydrate the body.

In addition to its intriguing health benefits, the recipe for chicken soup can easily be—and has been—adapted to local tastes. In her award-winning book *The Whole World Loves Chicken Soup*, food critic Mimi Sheraton details a wide range of delicious takes on the classic chicken soup recipe such as Arabian Red Lentil, Caribbean Pepper, Korean Samgyetang, and Congolese Muaumba Nsusu, made with palm oil and hot chili. Bet you can't wait to try some of these the next time you're feeling a little under the weather!

CHICKEN-FREE CHICKEN SOUP?

When the son of famous vegetarian Mahatma Gandhi was suffering from pneumonia and typhoid, Gandhi struggled with the physician's recommendation to feed him chicken soup. As his son's condition worsened, Gandhi relented to the "treatment" and his son did recover. Today, the anti-cold benefits of chicken-less chicken soup have yet to be formally studied, but many are happy with meat substitutes like tofu and vegan egg replacements, which are often made from tapioca starch and potato flour.

SPHERE

A sphere is a completely symmetrical three-dimensional-round object. A perfect sphere is completely symmetrical in relation to its center, with any point along its surface lying the same distance from the center point. The distance from the center to the surface is the sphere's radius. The diameter of a sphere is equal to twice the radius, and is equal to the maximum distance through the sphere in which a straight line can be drawn. A sphere has the largest volume of any shape given the same surface area. Unfortunately, a perfect sphere only exists in theory, because matter is composed of atoms, which are not "perfect." Perfect spheres would be useful in scientific fields like physics and space science, such as gravity probes for the National Aeronautics and Space Administration.

German mathematician David Hilbert, one of the founders of proof theory, a fundamental of mathematical logic, coauthored *Geometry and Imagination* with Stephan Cohn-Vossenis in 1932. Widely considered a classic and translated into English in 1952, it includes a section in which the authors observe eleven characteristics of a sphere. Three of these characteristics were completely unique to the sphere, meaning no other geometric shape shares these properties:

1. All the points on the sphere are the same distance from its center point.
2. All planes of a sphere and its contours are circles.
3. A sphere does not have a surface of centers.

The uniqueness and perfection of a sphere may only be relevant in science, but every day we use spheres that you probably never realized were "imperfect"—basketballs, soccer balls, pool balls, baseballs, and even ball bearings, and the tip of your ballpoint pen. But since so many sports use spheres, maybe the next time you miss a shot, you could explain to your coach how the ball is imperfect, not your game.

JUST A HAIR

In the May 2011 issue of *Nature*, researchers from Imperial College London's Centre for Cold Matter announced their conclusion to an almost ten-year study to accurately measure an electron, which seems to be *almost* a perfect sphere. How close to perfect? To within less than 0.000000000000000 000000000001cm. If you enlarged an electron to the size of the solar system, it would only be off-shape by the width of a human hair.

Perfect . . .

SPIRAL PASS

According to the University of Tennessee's physics department, a perfect spiral pass is a pass in which "the football spins about its symmetry axis, the football tilts during flight, so that its symmetry axis is tangent to its trajectory." The angular momentum and the relative velocity work together as nonparallel forces in the ball's trajectory. In simpler terms, as Super Bowl champion quarterback Drew Brees instructs on the show *Sport Science*, "To throw the perfect pass, it's all about the kinetic chain. It's now just a matter of that rhythm, of the energy being transferred from my feet, then to my hips, all the way up to my shoulders, and as my arm's coming through, the last thing to leave the ball is that index finger."

In an interesting experiment conducted on *Sport Science*, researchers set out to see who was more accurate: an NFL quarterback (Brees) or a professional archer. They had Brees make a twenty-yard (sixtyfoot) throw at a bull's-eye that was 4.8 inches in diameter, one-third of the circumference of the football's diameter, meaning the bull's-eye is three times smaller than the widest part of the football. *Sport Science* noted that only one in ten of the Olympic archers managed to hit the bull's-eye and that less than half of all the arrows shot in the 2008 Olympics landed on the bull's-eye. However, out of ten shots, Brees landed each one on the bull's-eye. And in addition to that, four out of those ten hit the bull's-eye of the bull's-eye, making him more accurate than the Olympic archer Badass for sure.

So, what's the secret of this perfect accuracy and spiral? The researchers at *Sport Science* outfitted a football with accelerometers to track and record the ball's movement and trajectory, and discovered that with slightly scary accuracy, Brees released the ball consistently each time at an angle of 6 degrees, and at a speed of 52 mph. When released, the football rotated along its long axis at almost 600 rpm, which is equivalent to the speed at which an air wrench spins the lugs off a NASCAR tire. The rotation creates a gyroscopic torque, and as gravity works to pull the nose of the ball downward, the aerodynamic forces of air flowing over the ball counterbalance each other to keep it on target.

Brees's ball has a slight wobble as it spins slightly off axis. These little wobbles—the shape the nose is tracing in the air—keep the ball on target. And Brees has just the right number of wobbles: three wobbles for every five rotations of the ball. So get out there and practice your spiral. You still may not make it into the NFL, but at least you'll be totally amazing at backyard ball.

STANDARDIZED TEST SCORE

*E*ducation and testing go hand in hand, and if you've gone to college or applied for grad school, you've likely faced the beast that is the standardized test. Standardized testing is big business, and despite criticism regarding the accuracy of what they claim to be assessing, these tests remain one of the best predictors for academic success. In addition to the well-known SAT, there are a variety of standardized tests with a variety of perfect scores, including:

- ACT: Originally stood for American College Testing. Perfect score: 36
- GMAT: Graduate Management Admission Test. Perfect score: 800
- GRE: Graduate Record Examinations. Perfect score: 1600
- LSAT: Law School Admission Test. Perfect score: 180
- MCAT: Medical College Admission Test. Perfect score: 45

How do each of these tests determine "perfect"? Read on.

SAT

The SAT debuted in 1926, and never left. Initially, SAT stood for "Scholastic Achievement Test," was later changed to "Scholastic Assessment Test," and while currently known as the SAT Reasoning

Test, the letters SAT no longer represent any actual words, making it an empty acronym. They could change the words to Suspicious Academic Treachery, or Sick Action Technology, and no one would blink. Everyone knows the SAT refers to the test you have to take to get into college and that it brands you with a set of numbers many keep more private than their Social Security number.

The SAT Reasoning Test includes three 800-point sections, which together make a perfect score of 2400, but since scoring is now based on percentiles, you don't have to get every question right to reach a perfect score. As long as you're in the 98.98th percentile, you're perfect—though 99 percent of the people you know might have a quibble with that. And if you're scratching your head a bit because you remember getting something like 1350 in the 1980s, and thought you did really well, it's because the third section wasn't added until 2005. For a long time, the perfect score was 1600.

ACT

American College Testing began usage in 1959, and tests skills in English, Mathematics, Reading, and Science, with an optional Writing test. The totals of the four main categories combine for the score, but the Writing test takers receive a separate score for that section, with a top possible score of 12. A perfect score is still considered a 36, though it could be said to be 36/12 to include the writing portion; however, since it's optional, it's not counted as a requirement for the traditional perfect score. In 2009, the average score (for the four sections) was 21.1.

GMAT

The Graduate Management Admission Test is taken by business students wishing to pursue a Master of Business Administration (MBA) degree. The test has three sections: Analytical Writing Assessment, the Quantitative section, and the Verbal Ability section. The writing essays are scored from zero to six, with zero being unintelligible and six being "outstanding." The Quantitative and Verbal sections are both worth zero to sixty points. The total score is taken from the Quantitative and Verbal sections and is graded on a curve, meaning that your final score depends on how well (or how poorly) your fellow test-takers did. (Analytical Writing is a completely separate score.) A perfect score is an 800, and the poorest score is 200. The median score for test takers in 2010 was 522. The average GMAT score of Harvard Business School students is 720, but many top business schools are happy with upper 600s.

GRE

The Graduate Record Examination is taken by students with Bachelor degrees before admission to school for Masters or Doctorate degrees. The sections of the test are: Verbal, Quantitative, Analytical Writing (with Issue Task and Argument Task), and an Experimental section comprised of new material the GRE is trying out; however, the test taker doesn't know which section is Experimental (and therefore not scored). Like the other tests, the Analytical Writing is scored separately than the rest of the test—a perfect score is a 6. The regular GRE score is much like the SAT—800 is the top score in Verbal and Quantitative and these top scores combine for the perfect score of 1600.

LSAT

The Law School Admission Test is taken by students intending to attend law school, and is taken all over the world. The score is taken from the combined score of the sections of Logical Reasoning, Reading Comprehension, Analytical Reasoning, and Writing. The LSAT also has a "Variable" category, which means that it includes an experimental section to determine questions for future tests. This section does not count toward the final score, and the test taker does not know what section won't be scored. The final score is determined by the raw scores of each category combining and being adjusted on a bell curve-like system that has small extremes and moves toward a median.

MCAT

The Medical College Admission Test is taken by students before they attend medical school. The four sections of the test are: Physical Science, Verbal Reasoning, Writing Sample, and Biological Sciences. All but the Writing section are multiple choice, and scored between one and fifteen. The Writing section is scored once by a computer, and once again by a human, on an alphabetical scale from J to T, with T being the perfect Writing score. The numerical scores (three sections of fifteen being the highest possible) are added together, making 45 the perfect numerical score, but if you include the Writing section, a perfect score is a 45T.

Standardized tests have never been more controversial since the passage of the No Child Left Behind Act of 2001, which mandated that schools must achieve certain scores in order to receive funding. Nicknamed "Every Child Left Behind" by teachers and administrators, these tests have caused even those professionals who are actively pro–standardized testing to turn up their noses.

In a 2007 interview with *Freakonomics*, W. James Popham, author of *The Truth About Testing: An Educator's Guide to Action*, describes the various forms of standardized tests as akin to French fries, ranging "from sublime to soggy." Popham refers to those tests as "misleading" and implores, "We definitely do need more standardized tests that are sufficiently sensitive to instructional quality."

Before you get up in arms about a poor score, bear in mind that generally the newer forms of testing bear the brunt of the criticism, while the old standards like the SAT and GRE are generally still held in esteem. However, while a perfect score is possible, a perfect *test* might not exist.

STORM

The perfect storm is used to describe a situation in which multiple events, although common enough on their own, come together in a rare display, creating a situation exponentially more intense that anyone would have initially foreseen. Its first known usage was in a Texas news piece from 1936, in which the Weather Bureau (the name at the time for the National Weather Service) explained that the cause of a flood involved seven different factors and that the "chain of circumstances" resulted in a "perfect storm." In describing the nor'easter that struck on Halloween of 1991, Bob Case, who was a deputy meteorologist in the Boston office of the National Weather Service at the time, explained that what would become perhaps the most famous of perfect storms was being caused by the convergence of three weather events: Hurricane Grace was bringing in tropical moisture from one direction; a low-pressure system was bringing warm air from another direction; and a high-pressure system was bringing cool and dry air from yet another.

As a series of events that dramatically heighten the danger of a situation, a perfect storm isn't relegated to only describing actual weather. A figurative "perfect storm" is used often in film and television, often with comedic purposes, with the worst possible combinations of characters and situations coming together to form a disaster.

An example of a popular film pitting characters and situations into a perfect storm for cringe-worthy comedy is Universal Pictures' 2000 film *Meet the Parents*.

So if you feel that everything is converging on you in exactly the wrong way, you may be experiencing a perfect storm of some kind, but at least not one caused by the weather . . . so, there's that to be thankful for!

THE *OTHER* HOLLYWOOD PERFECT STORM

Sebastian Junger's 1993 book *The Perfect Storm*, about the 1991 nor'easter that claimed the lives of several fishermen, brought the phrase "perfect storm" into common usage. The term became even more popular after the 2000 Warner Brothers film of the same name, but the film created a storm of its own: The surviving families of the very real fishermen who were lost in the nor'easter didn't appreciate the way the fictionalized fishermen were depicted as failing at their jobs and possibly greedy, and lawsuits and appeals ensued.

TEMPERATURE FOR SERVING RED WINE

$\mathcal{W}$ine requires that certain conditions be met—and quite often, so do the people who drink it. However, if you're a person who gets lost anywhere past Cab Sav or Merlot, the perfect temperature at which to serve red wine may have only briefly crossed your mind as you popped open that bottle after a hard day.

Wine expert Joseph Nase, who writes a wine column for *New York Magazine*, comes to the rescue with steps for making sure the wine you're serving is at the perfect temperature. But first you'll need a little background. At one time, Nase says, the temperature at which people drank red wine was largely determined by two factors:

1. The room temperature, which within castle walls would be somewhere in the low 60s (Fahrenheit)
2. The temperature of the wine cellar, which may have hovered around the mid 50s

Room temperatures today can be anywhere from the low 60s to mid 70s, and even higher in warm climates. Temperatures in the high 70s and above are not optimal for reds, so the standard advice of serving red wine at "room temperature" may not be the best. And let's face it, not many of us have wine cellars. To get your wines to their perfect respective temperatures, says Nase, conduct a mini experiment.

First, put a bottle of red wine in your fridge and leave it overnight. Next, use a thermometer and pour and taste the wine, first as it is cold, and then again several times as it slowly warms. Within hours you'll come to relate the way the taste corresponds to the different temperatures of the bottle, and will have the perfect gauge for any kind of red wine you'd like to serve.

WINE TEMPERATURE REFERENCE

PERFECT TEMPERATURE	WINE COLORS	TYPE OF WINES
60°F–65°F	Heavy Reds	Wines at their best in this range include full-bodied reds like Australian Shiraz, Bordeaux, California Cabernet Sauvignons and Merlots, Oregon Pinot Noirs, Italian Brunellos and Barolos, and Rhone Valley reds.
50°F–60°F	Lighter Reds	Lighter reds such as Chiantis, Riojas, Burgundies, and Pinot Noirs, as well as Loire Valley reds such as Bourgueil and Chinon. The bottle should begin feeling cold. Refrigerate for about an hour and a half.
Below 45°F	Boxed Reds	This is the temperature for wines with little complexity, where the nuances of taste are not paramount. Remove the wine from the refrigerator one hour before serving.

TEMPERATURE FOR SERVING WHITE WINE

*Y*ou may know that white wines are best served chilled, but how do you know when your wine is at the perfect temperature? It turns out that the glass of Chardonnay, Pinot Gris, or Riesling that you're drinking has likely been overchilled, as the average home refrigerator temperature is too low for many complex whites. Instead, try bringing that wine to the perfect temperature by placing the bottle in an ice bucket for twenty minutes. If you want to be even more specific in your quest for white wine perfection, try these very clear temperature suggestions from *New York Magazine* wine columnist Joseph Nase.

WINE TEMPERATURE REFERENCE

PERFECT TEMPERATURE	WINE COLORS	TYPE OF WINES
60°F–65°F	Blushes	The finest white Burgundy wines, like Montrachets, are best served in this range. The bottles should be cool to the touch. Refrigerate for around forty-five minutes.
50°F–60°F	Robust Whites	This includes most California and Australia Chardonnays, Auslese, and German Spatlese, as well as most white Burgundy wines. Good dessert wines such as late-harvest Rieslings and Sauternes are also good when served in this temperature range. The bottle should feel cool to the touch, and can be easily chilled in ice for ten to fifteen minutes.
45°F–50°F	Summery Whites	Light, fruity whites like those from the Loire, Bordeaux, and Alsace, as well as the lighter Australian whites, Oregon Pinot Gris, and all Sauvignon Blancs, will excel here. Bottle should be cold to the touch. Chill in the fridge for two hours. Ice wine and vintage champagne also belong here.
Below 45°F	Rosés	This is the temperature for wines with little complexity, such as lower-quality sweet wines, nonvintage sparkling wines and rosés, and basic Spanish and Portuguese whites. Ice cold. Chilled in the fridge for three hours.

TIME TO HAVE A CUP
OF COFFEE

*S*o many people have their cup of coffee first thing in the morning, almost as soon as their feet hit the floor. But the perfect time to have a cup of coffee is actually after you've been awake for a few hours, not first thing.

Using caffeine to stay awake is effective, but the way most of us use it is not. The typical approach to ward off daytime sleepiness is to slam two, three, or even four cups of coffee at the start of the day. Unfortunately, in doing so you're setting yourself up for a long, drawn-out caffeine crash over the course of the day. That's because there are two processes going on that control your sleep cycle, and they work in opposition to each other. The circadian system is your rhythmic internal clock, releasing hormones (like melatonin) that push for sleep cyclically (it's activated by darkness), not continually. The other process is a homeostatic system that increasingly pushes for sleep the longer you're awake.

The critical chemical in the homeostatic system is adenosine, which steadily builds up in your system over the course of the day, beginning when you wake up. It's at its lowest levels while your circadian rhythm is pushing you the hardest to stay awake. Much like melatonin releases at night, adenosine builds up to be at a greater level at night as well.

Caffeine binds to the receptors for adenosine, so ingesting caffeine pushes back at the force that is increasingly trying to put you to sleep, as the adenosine is effectively blocked from (a portion of) its receptors. That is why it's best to have a cup of coffee after you've been awake a few hours, rather than when you wake up. By having coffee later, you are using your stay-awake weapon, caffeine, at the same time that your body has begun to produce more adenosine. You want to choose your time for caffeine carefully, as too much caffeine in receptors will signal the adrenal gland of a problem, and that's when you get a racing heartbeat and increased blood flow, which will actually make you more tired. The optimal way to use caffeine, then, is to slowly build the levels of caffeine in your body at the same time that the adenosine is building.

A 2004 study by Rush University Medical Center, Brigham and Women's Hospital, and Harvard Medical school confirms that people who take frequent but small amounts of caffeine at regular intervals over the course of the day not only stay awake and perform well cognitively, but find that unlike those who have a full cup of coffee late in the day, the caffeine doesn't mess with their sleep cycle.

Dr. James Wyatt, a sleep researcher involved with the study through Rush University, stated in a press release: "I hate to say it, but most of the population is using caffeine the wrong way by drinking a few mugs of coffee or tea in the morning." *Small amounts* are the key words here, so the caffeine can slowly and gently block receptors, just as the adenosine is slowly and gently growing through the day. Large amounts, like Dr. Wyatt mentioned, do lead to tired adrenals and a "crash," though people feeling the initial lift from that first cup are apt to keep drinking cup after cup for more lift. So all those people nursing that one to two cups throughout the duration of the day, even after it's turned cold, have been cleverly adopting the best scientific practices all along.

TIME TO USE FOUL
LANGUAGE

*N*owadays, bad language is popping up everywhere. People drop the F-bomb on the subway, in music, and in movies, and some curse words can now be said on television. However, the perfect time to swear is actually when you're in pain. According to a study conducted by Richard Stephens and Claudia Umland from Keele University's School of Psychology and published in *The Journal of Pain,* the impulse to immediately belt out an obscenity or two after stubbing your toe may serve a useful purpose: It numbs the pain. The catch is that it only works for people who rarely curse. Stephens and Umland found that test subjects who don't normally swear were able to hold their hands in a bowl of ice water for 70 seconds if they said neutral words, like "rabbit" or "dandelion." But when they uttered swear words, the amount of time they were able to leave their hands in the ice water jumped to 140 seconds.

Subjects who were "swearers" and used curse words on a regular basis were able to keep their hands in the ice water for 120 seconds while using neutral words, but when they did let lose their usual torrent, it produced no benefit. They had the same 120-second tolerance.

The researchers believe the act of swearing triggers what they call "stress-induced analgesia," which along with an increase in adrenaline is a natural method of pain relief tied into our fight-or-flight response. Stephens suggests that, when used sparingly, swearing can provide short-term, but immediate, pain relief in situations where you have few, if any, other options. The problem comes when you have become desensitized to the power of swearing and your words of fire have lost most of their pain-relieving heat. So when your teachers or parents said you shouldn't swear because it made your vocabulary look limited, they could actually have made a more compelling argument by saying that reserving your swears could help you with pain relief!

Perfect . . .

TOWN TO LIVE IN THE UNITED STATES

When people think about the perfect place to live, many of them see white picket fences, a green grassy lawn, and neighbors who wave at each other when they get home from work. Does this perfect place exist? According to _CNNMoney_, this little slice of heaven can be found in Louisville, Colorado.

Louisville was rated on multiple subcategories within the categories of:

- Financial well-being
- Housing
- Education
- Quality of life
- Leisure and culture
- Weather
- "Meet the neighbors," which included education level, marriage rates, and ages

While Louisville's population is only 18,400, it enjoys close proximity to the city of Denver, giving its residents access to the positives of a city without being stuck in one.

Louisville enjoys low crime and unemployment rates as well as an excellent range of jobs in fields like aerospace, clean energy, and employment staples like tech and health care. The Rockies provide endless recreational activities that vary with the season, and real estate prices "have barely budged since 2005."

For you city mice out there who have already dismissed the idea of a suburb, *Parenting* chose Washington, D.C., as the best city in which to raise a family, based on eighty-four different categories, such as crime rates, employment rates, and kiddie-friendly factors like parks, museums, and the best schools. *Parenting* points out D.C.'s great places for family meals, recreational activities, and seemingly endless museums —there are forty-four of them, to be exact. If you remember the 1990s, you might still think of a crack-smoking mayor and the dubious distinction of "Murder Capital of the United States," but in fact, according to data from the Federal Bureau of Investigation, since 1995 violent crime in D.C. has decreased by 50 percent and property crime is down 49.8 percent. The runner-up according to *Parenting* was Austin, Texas, for the second year in a row. Austin was also the number one "Best City for the Next Decade" according to *Kiplinger's Personal Finance Magazine* in 2010, and ranked number eight in *CNNMoney's* 2011 "10 Fastest-Growing Cities."

WORST PLACES TO LIVE
IN THE UNITED STATES

The "U.S. Misery Index" has existed since the time of President Lyndon Johnson, and can be found at *www.miseryindex .us*. It doesn't report specific towns, but highlights some issues you'll find in the worst places. According to *AOL Daily Finance*, the "Worst Place to Live" is El Centro, California, but according to *Forbes*, Stockton, California, is "The Most Miserable City" in the United States. In addition, *CBS News* rated Hawaii as "The Worst State to Make a Living" in 2011.

VACATION

*E*veryone loves vacation. Whether you're sitting on a beach in the Caribbean or taking a cruise to see glaciers in Alaska, it truly can be the most wonderful time of the year. But what makes a vacation perfect? An article in the *New York Times* interviewed experts and examined behavioral research studies to discover the ingredients of the perfect vacation. The various experts interviewed found a variety of factors that contribute to strategizing the perfect vacation.

Anticipation

Enjoy this, because it might be the best part. A 1997 study by psychologists Terence Mitchell of the University of Washington and Leah Thompson of Northwestern University investigated the experiences of travelers during three phases of their vacations: anticipation, the vacation itself, and how they remembered it. The study found people were happier during the anticipation stage than when they were actually on the vacation.

A 2010 study by Jeroen Nawijn, research lecturer at Breda University of Applied Sciences in the Netherlands, had the same findings, with almost two-thirds of participants reporting their greatest level of happiness during the anticipation of the vacation.

Short Is Fine

Nawijn told the *New York Times*, "I found that the length of stay has very little influence on how people feel during a trip or afterwards." (You may feel relieved that Professor Nawijn isn't scheduling your vacation time, but on average the Dutch have more paid vacation days than do Americans.) Nawijn says it's about balance, since you don't want to spend too many of your vacation days each year traveling rather than enjoying your leisure time.

Make the Most of It

Al Gini, a business ethics professor at Loyola University of Chicago and the author of *The Importance of Being Lazy*, points out that you can't flip a switch to suddenly relax, and that it can often take a week just to decompress and start to get into the rhythm of time off. Gini says the solution is to begin slowing down before you go, rather than working full force and often frantically right up to the day you're going to leave. If possible—and if you have an understanding boss—give yourself a few days of not working full blast at work, and take some leisurely time to pack and prepare. He advised the same goes for the end of the trip; rather than spending your last days of vacation racing around sightseeing, spend the last few days of your trip relaxing and "lounging by the pool."

To Connect or Not

Communication technology has exploded with such force over the past decade, it has yet to be determined what the best course of action is when on vacation. New York University's dean of social sciences, Dalton Conley, found that some people can actually become more stressed if they're not connected, as they worry about what could be going wrong, or what they're missing out on. Others find ways to rejoice in the rarity of being offline. In his 2009 book *Elsewhere, U.S.A.*, Conley calls the ever-blurring line between work and leisure "weisure." If you're one of those who will lose their sanity without a connection, the suggestion is to make a specific time to check in, and stick with it. And if you'd like to let it all go but have the connection compulsion, take a vacation to an "unplugged" place where you won't have a choice.

Cover Your Back

Joe Kissell at Macworld.com Business Center recommends you set up your e-mail with its automatic out-of-office reply option, even if you might be checking your e-mail while on your trip, just to keep yourself covered. Make sure it clearly states your return date. Kissell also recommends the same for your voice mail, and reminds that if you are tempted to set up a service that sends voice mail to e-mail, the day right before you leave on vacation is not the time for a new tech undertaking.

Practice Immersion

Find activities on vacation that fully draw you in and keep you busy. Several studies, such as research done by Elizabeth Dunn from the University of Columbia and Christopher Hsee of the University of Chicago Booth School of Business, have shown that active people are happier than those who are inactive. This doesn't mean that you should maintain a frenetic pace on vacation. Hsee suggests, for example, that if you're in Italy, you might take an Italian cooking class instead of eating out. If you're in Mexico, you could try taking an archaeological tour instead of scheduling endless resort days.

Have a Finale

Nobel laureate and Princeton psychologist Daniel Kahneman has found what he calls the "peak-end rule." When you look back on your vacation, how you feel about it depends most on the peaks. While you can't force such things to happen at the end of your trip, planning something special toward the end of the trip can be enough to end it perfectly.

VACUUM

*A*t some point, there may have been someone knocking on your door to tell you about a perfect vacuum, but it's doubtful they were talking about space without matter, which is how science defines the term. So what is a vacuum? Well, a vacuum is a space that is empty, so when it comes to cleaning, the vacuum sucked away the molecules of dirt from a space, and in terms of science, in a vacuum *everything* has been sucked out, including the air. As of now, the perfect vacuum is only a theoretical concept, as humans have yet to experience a lack of matter.

The creation of a vacuum is the reason that everything goes haywire when an airplane door is opened at high altitude. The air pressure is significantly lower outside the plane than inside. If a door is opened, the pressurized air rushing out to fill the low pressure is what causes chaos. Residential vacuum cleaners can decrease air pressure by around 20 percent, which is strong enough suck in loose corn flakes and cat hair but too weak to separate the molecules in your floor and create a tear in the space-time continuum. It's merely a low vacuum, and no matter what the salesman said, it's not perfect.

Science can get close to a perfect vacuum, but the problems lie in the particles, like electron pairs, coming off a container used to contain the "nothing." And then there are the random and theoretical factors, like the presence of theoretical dark matter, or virtual particles that only exist for a certain time in a certain space. A perfect vacuum should also have a temperature of zero degrees Kelvin, which is also known as "absolute zero," a theoretical temperature in which no thermal kinetic energy exists within molecules. And if there are zero molecules of dirt left on your rug after you vacuum, it seems justified to describe *that* as a perfect vacuum as well.

Perfect . . .

VIEW OF SPACE

*M*an has been looking up at the sky trying to decipher its meanings since time immemorial—but it's fairly certain they weren't doing that from the perfect place on Earth from which to view space: the inhospitable Antarctic Plateau, at a little over 13,000 feet above sea level. Researchers say it's one of the coldest, calmest, and driest locations on earth, with an average temperature of –94°F, almost no wind, and a water content in the atmosphere "sometimes less than the thickness of a human hair," says study author Dr. Will Saunders.

The site was discovered in 2009 by a joint American-Australian research team examining all factors that come into play for creating the best conditions for studying the sky, such as: water vapor, brightness, cloud cover, temperature, wind speed, and atmospheric "turbulence."

The team studied information gathered by ground observations, climate models, and satellite images to assess the perfection of the site for viewing space. Focus has intensified on Antarctica as a potentially prime location for astronomical observatories after a 2004 paper published in *Nature* observed that a ground-based telescope was capable of capturing images almost of the same quality as those from the space-based Hubble telescope.

According to Dr. Saunders of the Anglo-Australian Observatory, who also is a visiting professor at the University of New South Wales, the images they'll be able to take from a site called Ridge A within the Australian Antarctic Territory will be, at a minimum, three times sharper than currently possible from even the best sites elsewhere. "Because the sky there is so much drier and darker, it means that a modestly-sized telescope there would be as powerful as the largest telescopes anywhere else on earth," explains Dr. Saunders.

But before you pack up your thermal long johns to gawk at the galaxy—remember that the observatory doesn't exist yet. While an earth-based telescope is far cheaper than a space-based one such as the Hubble, the harsh terrain makes it a pricey operation, and the teams are still awaiting funding.

Too Cold to Hold

The Antarctic Plateau does not support any forms of life—there aren't any plants, animals, or even microorganisms. On occasion, birds are "blown" in, but usually freeze to death. Occasionally some microorganisms come in on humans visiting the area for exploration or research, but they are not able to thrive. The coasts of Antarctica are able to host some ocean-dependent life such as seabirds, penguins, and seals, but no sizable land animals can survive there.

Perfect . . .

VOICE

Throughout history, there have been voices that seem to be heaven sent, but what makes a great voice perfect? Linguist Andrew Linn of Sheffield University and sound engineer Shannon Harris created a mathematical formula to define the perfect human voice:

PVQ = ([164.2wpm x 0.48pbs]Fi)

In this equation:

- PVQ stands for Perfect Voice Quality
- Wpm is words per minute
- Pbs is pauses between sentences
- Fi is falling intonation

The timing of the speech was important. Linn and Harris found that the ideal voice should not speak more than 164 words per minute. A 0.48 of a second pause between sentences was the preferred timing. Falling intonation means that as a sentence progressed, the words should fall in intonation. (For a rise in intonation, think "Valley Girls"— a way of speaking that makes everything sound like a question? So yeah, that's like, the opposite of perfect?)

Positive characteristics are consciously or subliminally associated with certain vocal traits, which were also a part of the study. Linn found that the positive traits most valued in a voice were those that exuded "confidence and trust." The study also included panelists gauging their "emotional response" to voices. "The results of this study give us an exciting look into the way voices work and what makes them appealing or repelling," Linn said.

A spokesperson for the study said, "All the voices analyzed were British. There might be some cultural component but it should apply to all foreign languages." The top-scoring female voices were:

- Actress Dame Judi Dench
- Television reporter Mariella Frostup
- Actress Honor Blackman

The top-scoring men were actors were Alan Rickman and Jeremy Irons, or as the average moviegoer may know them, Professor Severus Snape and Simba's Uncle Scar. Perfect? You be the judge.

TURN IT TO LOW

William Shakespeare said "Speak low, if you speak love," in "Much Ado About Nothing," but it turns out a lower-pitched voice *is* used by both men and women when they speak to someone to whom they're attracted, according to a study from Albright College and the University of Baltimore. The study also found "individuals also tend to raise the pitch of their voices when attempting to deceive another person." A lower pitch intends to convey the opposite to a potential lover.

Perfect . . .

WAY TO BLOW YOUR NOSE

*Y*ou have a head cold. You have the sniffles. You have seasonal allergies. You're constantly blowing your nose. But are you practicing perfection every time that you pluck a tissue from the box? It depends on how you're blowing.

University of Virginia researchers studying pediatric infectious diseases, led by Dr. J. Owen Hendley, have determined that blowing your nose has the potential to cause damage, but not if you blow your nose with the right technique. Subjects in the study were monitored as they blew their noses, coughed, and sneezed. In addition to observing subjects with CT scans, some lucky subjects had an opaque dye inserted into their rear nasal cavities. Hendley found that although the coughing and sneezing created little or no pressure in the nasal cavity, nose blowing was more dramatic. Each time they blew their nose, subjects produced a fairly tremendous amount of pressure—the same you'd see in a reading of someone's diastolic or resting blood pressure—that forced mucus back into their sinuses. Hendley theorizes the extreme backward pressure could send bacteria or viruses into the sinuses and lead to additional infection.

The technique to employ, according to Dr. Anil Kumar Lalwani, the chairman of the Department of Otolaryngology (ear, nose, and throat) at the New York University Langone Medical Center, is to blow your nose one nostril at a time, which keeps the pressure buildup to a minimum. Harvard Medical School also recommends the one-nostril-at-a-time method, as does ABC's *Good Morning America*. The next time you feel a sneeze coming on, grab a tissue . . . and achieve a little bit of perfection.

SNEEZE-INDUCED INJURY

Until his big sneeze, the thirty-five-year-old anonymous patient had been healthy, but right after sneezing an intense pain developed in his neck for ten minutes. As the pain eased, he was left with partial paralysis and loss of feeling on his left side. Doctors later determined he had suffered an aneurysm in his neck as a result of the sneeze, which in turn deprived a section of his spinal cord of blood, and that in turn led to nerve damage.

Perfect . . .

WAY TO BRUSH YOUR TEETH

ooth brushing may seem like a minor part of your health routine, but recent studies have linked major health problems like heart attacks to gum disease. Dr. Mehmet Oz revealed on *Good Morning America* that many people don't know how to brush their teeth. To make sure your teeth are as perfect as they can be, try the following routine, which is recommended by the American Dental Hygienists' Association (ADHA).

Note: To keep from damaging or irritating your gums, use a soft nylon brush with rounded-end bristles.

1. Hold your toothbrush so the bristles are at a 45-degree angle along your gumline. The bristles should be in contact with the tooth surface and your gums.
2. Use a pea-sized amount of toothpaste. Brush the outer surfaces of two to three teeth at a time, and use alternating motions of back, forward, and circles, then shift to the next two to three teeth and do the same.
3. Continuing to keep the head of the brush at a 45-degree angle, and in contact with both the gumline and tooth surface, use the same method as above for brushing the inside surfaces of your teeth.

4. When it comes to your front teeth, both top and bottom, pivot the brush so it's vertical, like you are biting into the bristles. Using the front half of the brush, use repeated up-and-down motions to clean the inside surfaces.

5. Gently clean of the top surfaces your teeth, the places food first touches, with a back-and-forth scrubbing motion. Don't be too vigorous or you'll have some irritation and eventually gum erosion. Last, scrub the top surface of your tongue to remove bacteria.

Tooth brushing done this way should last a full two minutes. Both the ADHA and Dr. Oz recommend that at minimum you should replace your toothbrush every three months, as toothbrushes can easily harbor over 10,000,000 bacteria. Besides changing your brush frequently, store the brush at least six feet away from the toilet, to avoid airborne microbes. If you don't have a toothbrush handy, you can break up plaque with a swish of green tea. Coffee and black teas also work to break up plaque, but are more staining.

WAY TO CHOP AN ONION

*I*f you tear up every time you chop an onion, don't feel bad. You're not alone. The reason for the tearing involves vacuoles (an organelle bound by a membrane) within the onion, which individually hold enzymes and sulfur-containing compounds the onion has derived from the soil. When you cut into the onion, you cut across the vacuoles, and the sulfur compounds and enzymes come into contact with each other. The enzymes begin breaking down the sulfur molecules into smaller molecules, small enough that they become volatile and start to rise. The sulfur compound reaching toward you isn't so bad, but as it reacts with the moisture in your eyes, it forms a fairly unholy threesome of sulfuric acid, hydrogen sulfide, and sulfur dioxide.

Soaking onions before you chop can take away their tear-making power, advises food and cooking site Epicurious.com. This method dilutes the eye-irritating compounds, so to allow the water to get at them, cut the onion in half before soaking.

Refrigerating an onion or chilling it in ice water will leave the reaction-causing enzyme sluggish, putting some brakes on the process of the sulfur compound breaking down and turning volatile. Also, the highest concentration of sulfur-containing compounds is in the root end of the onion. Instead of cutting both top and bottom, just cut off the top and peel the outer layers, leaving the root end as it is.

An Inaccurate Science

Here's a trick taught at Parisian chef and instructor Paule Caillat's cooking classes in Paris: Put a piece of bread in your mouth to prevent onion-inspired tears. The science behind it might be unproven, but her students swear by it.

Perfect . . .

WAY TO COOL YOUR MOUTH

*I*n many restaurants and homes around the country, hot sauce is king. People are now scared of sriracha, start sweating when they order something containing Scotch Bonnet, and tremble at the appearance of a ghost pepper. Today some restaurants even offer sauces or salsas so hot that the diner is required to sign a waiver before they'll be served.

How can you decide whether or not to try a particular pepper? It's pretty simple. The heat of peppers is measured in Scoville units. The green and red bell peppers you come across on a crudités platter fall in the harmless range of 100 to 1,000 Scoville units, while hot peppers like jalapeño, cayenne, and habanero (the hottest) range from a mild hot at 5,000 Scoville units up to a nuclear winter at 300,000 Scoville units. There's an urban legend identifying the seeds in peppers as the source of the heat, but the true cause is an oil found in the veins of the peppers called capsaicin. The more capsaicin, the more Scoville units.

And the reason hot peppers can leave your mouth feeling like someone just dropped it on the grill? Because according to the neurotransmitters in your brain, someone did. Your mouth is sending messages to mission control that it's been set on fire, and in response your brain releases a salvo of heat-tempering behaviors—your nose starts running, your eyes start tearing, and the sweat won't stop. Thankfully, there's something called a "transient receptor potential cation channel subfamily V member 1," or TRPV1 for short. TRPV1 is a heat-regulating protein that kicks in within the temperature range of 98.6°F to 113°F. In 1997, a University of California–San Francisco research team discovered that capsaicin selectively binds to TRPV1 and causes the protein to go to work even at the normal body temperature of 98.6°F, causing your heat and pain neurons to start firing. The result is that although it *feels like* you could fry an egg on your tongue, in reality you'd just have a cold, wet, and very raw egg in your mouth.

So you take a bite of pepper and the capsaicin binds to and activates TRPV1, triggering the sensation of heat. When it's too hot to handle, what do you grab for relief? The tall glass of ice water? Definitely not. Remember that capsaicin is an oil, and as such is not water soluble. Flood your mouth with water, and there might be a moment of bliss, and then your tongue and mouth will realize the water didn't wash anything off, it just spread the capsaicin all over. Now everything is burning. Fortunately, to find relief all you have to do is take a big swig of milk or other dairy product.

Casein, a substance found in milk, will mix with capsaicin, dissolve it, and help wash it away. Any dairy product will do in a pinch, but swishing a mouthful of milk in five-second intervals is probably the easiest and most effective antidote for capsaicin. The perfect solution!

WAY TO CRACK AN EGG

Have you ever gone to crack an egg and ended up with a handful of yolk? Does it seem as though, sometimes, more egg ends up on your table than in the bowl? Well, the perfect way to crack an egg is to hold it in your nondominant hand (if you're right-handed, hold it in your left) with the egg's pointy end pointing toward the ends of your fingers. Then, with the same motion as casting a yo-yo—or the way you would crack a whip if that's more your style—bring down an artist's palette knife across the middle of the egg. In studies, this technique with the palette knife brought just the right amount of pressure to make a clean break, while keeping the cracking to either side of the strike line minimal, and consequently offered the least chance of ending up with shell in your mix.

This egg-cracking method is a far cry from the one-handed version wherein the egg is palmed by a super confident television chef who continues to talk as he strikes the egg against the edge of the pan in one swift motion, gracefully splitting the two sides of the shell apart through some magical trick involving the thumb and pinky. You didn't even have to look to know that sitting in the bottom of the pan was the perfect egg, its unbroken yolk as bright as the sun. Generally the end result of that method for us laypeople is a smashed yolk and a bowlful of shell shards.

With a thickness of just 0.5mm—less than 1/16 inch—eggshells are fairly delicate, and making clean cracks that leave the yolk intact with the egg free of shell fragments can be difficult. Scientists investigating the issue methodically went through hundreds of eggs and employed just about any kitchen utensil that offered even a glimmer of promise. Researchers also had to account for all the variables.

Professor Sally Solomon with Glasgow University led the research team within the Poultry Research Unit, which involves actual scientists and not hilarious hijinks with Foghorn Leghorn. "There are many factors involved in getting the perfect break," Solomon told *The Telegraph* in its issue of March 1, 2001, "the type of implement, velocity, angle of impact, force, and a good follow-through motion." Part of the reason it's so difficult to get the perfect break is that the shell is composed of several layers, and the strength of these is dependent upon not just the age and health of the hen that laid the egg, but also the way the egg has been stored as it went from hen to you. Solomon's team arrived at the method giving the best and most reliable break: the palette-knife method.

Still, even the best technique can be foiled by variables beyond your control. Larger eggs and eggs that have been stored for a while are more prone to cracking, and the membrane that protects the yolk is also less strong. In the end, your best bet for the best cracking of the best eggs is to use eggs that are medium sized—not large, extra large, jumbo, or supersized—and fresh. Once in your possession, the ideal environment for eggs is in the fridge, in a box, at a consistent temperature.

Scooping Shells

The trick to extricating shell bits when they've already slipped into the bowl is to use another piece of shell. One of the empty half-shells will work perfectly. Just like the first piece that got in, the sharp edge of the half-shell will easily cut through the gel that cushions the yolk, rather than just pushing the gel around.

Perfect . . .

WAY TO DE-SKUNK
YOUR DOG

The first time your dog comes back to you after having been skunked, your definition of smelly will be significantly broadened. Fortunately, remedies abound claiming to effectively separate your dog from the smell, but since common methods like tomato-juice baths leave the dogs continuing to smell, you might begin to suspect that the perfect solution doesn't exist. The good news is that you would be incorrect.

In 1993, chemist Paul Krebaum discovered a solution, described as perfect by lovers of skunked pets. Unfortunately for him, he's not able to make a mint bottling the recipe, because the ingredients responsible for eliminating the smell of skunk are impossible to bottle. Put hydrogen peroxide, baking soda, and some dish soap together in a bottle and it will explode. Separately, it's completely safe. Krebaum and William Wood of Humboldt State University shared the following method on the NPR radio show *Talk of the Nation* on April 24, 2009. The program shared the story of Annette Heist, host of *Science Friday*, using this method to great success with her dog Pete. "Aside from the five oxidizing baths, Pete came out of this unscathed, but he has no idea how lucky he is," Heist said, noting that the old folk remedy of tomato juice "does not work!"

Krebaum's Skunk Remedy

1 quart of 3 percent hydrogen peroxide. The 3 percent solution is usually sold in pint (500ml) bottles, so you'll need to pick up two of them. Krebaum suggests using only the 3 percent grade, which is usually marked "USP," as it meets certain standards for both purity and medical use. Using other percentages of peroxide can prove dangerous—even if you're a chemist.

¼ cup of baking soda. Be certain you've selected baking *soda*, and not baking *powder*. While they may seem similar, they behave quite differently. Baking soda is also referred to as sodium bicarbonate; it's sodium *bicarbonate* that you need, not sodium *carbonate*. Verify that you *don't have* sodium carbonate, which is also called washing soda. Washing soda is roughly a hundred times more alkaline than baking soda, and will cause skin burns to both you and your dog.

1 to 2 teaspoons of liquid soap. Krebaum says two brands are preferable, Softsoap and Ivory Liquid. He has no affiliation with either, but the surfactant package in both is mostly inert, and so will cause the peroxide to auto-decompose (into water) the least. Products marketed as "heavy duty" and "grease cutting," such as Dawn, will have a more negative impact, and the worst choice would be shampoo.

1. Mix the ingredients together in a clean plastic bucket, and use clean plastic utensils as well, since metals will trigger the peroxide to start breaking down. Use the solution as soon as possible after mixing it. Once mixed, the peroxide will begin to slowly break down into oxygen and water, making the solution less effective.

2. In order to fully cover a larger pet, you can increase the amount of solution by adding a quart of lukewarm water.

3. Get to work washing your pet, making sure to work the solution deep into its coat. Let the solution sit for about five minutes or until the smell is gone. If your pet has been sprayed in the face, do your best to keep the solution out of his eyes, as it will sting. Krebaum suggests that if you have any cuts on your hands, you can protect them by wearing latex gloves.

4. When you're done with the washing, rinse off your pet *thoroughly* with lukewarm water.

5. Pour any leftover solution you have down the drain with running water. If you start thinking about saving what you have left, stop and remember the catch: If you store this solution in a closed container it will begin producing pressure, and will continue to do so until it blows.

It's worth repeating. Never, ever, *ever*, enclose the solution in a container of any kind. To further drive the point home, Krebaum gives the following answer to anyone wondering just how much pressure the peroxide solution will actually produce as it decomposes: It will depend on how full the container is, but a bottle half-full of the solution will produce around 140 pounds per square inch (psi), and a bottle three-quarters full will produce 420 psi. To sum up: A clean-smelling dog = perfect. An explosion inside your house = not so much.

Perfect . . .

WAY TO ESTIMATE THE
NUMBER OF M&M'S IN
A CONTAINER

*Y*ou may think that guessing the correct number of M&M's in the jar at the fair, so you can win the pink stuffed tiger, is a complete and total crapshoot. First you look at the jar and think, I have absolutely no idea, how could I even guess the number? But then maybe you come up with your own mathematical formula. You guess there's maybe sixty M&M's bags, maybe 200 M&M's in each bag? Another quick mental calculation and you realize it's all just wild guessing any way you slice it.

Thanks to some researchers at Princeton University, however, you now have a fighting chance. For years, scientists have been investigating how densely identical spheres can be packed in order to make the most efficient use of space. Books, for example, with their systematic rectangular shape, can be carefully arranged and efficiently packed in cardboard. But when randomly dropped in the same box, very few fit. Most often in these guessing games, the container has been randomly filled, not packed. Further, it's often been assumed that for the densest packing in a random fill, the best shape is that of a sphere.

Randomly arranged spheres will take up around 68 percent of the available space in a container.

Using this formula, estimate as best you can, in cubic centimeters, the volume of the jar. Multiply this by 0.68, while silently congratulating yourself on having brought along your smartphone, and then divide this number by 0.636—the volume of one plain M&M's candy. Then give that pink tiger a good squeeze.

Perfect . . .

WAY TO LACE YOUR SHOES

Mathematician Dr. Burkard Polster, of the Monash University in Victoria, Australia, would like to set you straight on the notion that there are only a couple of ways to lace a pair of shoes. He's found that the average shoe with a row of six eyelets on either side of the tongue can be laced in 43,200 unique ways. While not every method results in something pretty and many produce tangles, each will functionally keep the two sides of the shoe together. Despite all of these options (and one hopes at least some of this was simulated and he didn't physically run through all 43,200 methods), most of the world follows one of these two perfect pathways:

1. The most prevalent method is the basic crisscross, in which each end of the lace goes from one eyelet on one side to the next eyelet on the opposite side.
2. The other technique is the one in which one end of the lace is passed from the last eyelet on one side, across to the uppermost eyelet on the opposite side, and then the other end is woven through the eyelets in a zigzagged "N" pattern.

These are the most common methods for good reason—they happen to be the two strongest possible ways to lace your shoes. However, each is better suited to a certain eyelet configuration. When the eyelets are spaced closely together but the two opposing flaps are relatively far apart, the crisscross is superior. The tension of the crisscross pattern is strongest horizontally, and brings the two sides together. When the eyelets are spaced farther apart, the "N" pattern held the best.

Of course, Velcro is always an option if this sounds a little too complicated.

COMING UP SHORT

If you end up with a shoelace that's just barely long enough, or a shoelace that's been broken, then you should employ what Burkard Polster refers to as the "bow tie," which makes the most efficient use of length while still keeping your shoe tied together. You pass the lace from one eyelet to the next eyelet on the same side, and then cross diagonally to the other side.

Perfect . . .

WAY TO POUR CHAMPAGNE

*I*n December of 1662, English naturalist Christopher Merret presented the Royal Society with his paper *Some Observations Concerning the Ordering of Wines*, in which he described the process of adding molasses and sugar to wines already in the bottle—intentionally creating a second fermentation process that made wine "drink brisk and sparkling." But Champagne would belong to the French, and only the sparkling wine produced in the Champagne region of France can properly be called "Champagne." Sparkling wine produced anywhere else in the world (including elsewhere in France) is just sparkling wine, in accordance with various regulations and international treaty. So it is only fitting that a study demonstrating the conditions for a perfectly poured glass comes from France's Champagne region.

When poured in the traditional method, from a bottle held vertically into a fluted glass that's standing straight up, Champagne develops a thick foam head, which rises quickly and then reduces gradually. That foam pattern is all too familiar to anyone who has poured a beer directly into a glass. To prevent the excess foaming, beer is poured into a glass at an angle, reducing the head.

Researchers from the University of Reims, led by Gerard Liger-Belair, Guillaume Polidori, and Clara Cilindre, used infrared imaging to measure carbon dioxide (CO_2) loss from Champagne as it was poured. In the *Journal of Agriculture and Food Chemistry*, they released their findings about the perfect pour: Champagne poured into the glass at an angle, similar to beer, was less volatile and lost less gas than Champagne poured straight. It also best retained its flavor and fizz. Earlier research had shown that the more CO_2 bubbles remaining in Champagne after it's been poured, the better the taste.

Bubbles also are best preserved when Champagne is served at colder temperatures. At 40°F, Champagne poured in the traditional way lost 25 percent of its CO_2, and just half that when poured at an angle. Regardless of pouring method, Champagne served near room temperature quickly went flat. Its ideal serving temperature is between 45°F and 48°F.

PUT A CORK IN IT

Benedictine monk Dom Pierre Pérignon has often been credited with the discovery of Champagne. However, he didn't exactly "discover" it. He was directed by his superiors at the Abbey of Hautvillers to find a way to prevent the unintended second fermentation that would occur, as it caused their bottles to explode, so he came up with the idea to wire the cork to the bottle to prevent the corks from popping during fermentation. Which didn't actually stop the second fermentation, but you know how those monks will twist any story for good press.

WAY TO SHOVEL SNOW

Shoveling snow is a difficult workout, but for some people, it's unavoidable. Ken Hellevang, an agricultural engineer at North Dakota State University, says the weight of snow will vary by type. A cubic foot of fluffy snow might weigh around seven pounds, more average snow maybe fifteen pounds, and compacted snow can weigh twenty pounds or more per cubic foot. If it's turning to ice the weight will increase dramatically.

The Canadian Centre for Occupational Health and Safety says that the perfect shoveling rate is fifteen scoops per minute, and at that rate each scoop lifted should be no heavier than ten to fifteen pounds. If you're shoveling slower, more weight can be added, but you should not exceed twenty-four pounds per lift. Loads between ten to fifteen pounds should be tossed no higher than four feet and no farther than three feet; if logistics require more distance, the load should be lightened.

Roy Berendsohn, the senior home editor of *Popular Mechanics*, has some cardinal rules for the perfect snow-shoveling job:

- **Stretch.** Recognize that shoveling is physical work, and treat it that way. Stretch your back, shoulders, and hamstrings. Rather than a sprint, treat it like a marathon, and work your way into a comfortable groove. Maintain good posture.

223

- **Move snow once.** Don't shovel snow onto areas you are going to have to shovel later. Before starting, survey the scene and choose your dumping sites. Toss your first shovelfuls farther away from you, so you don't quickly build up a mound right next to you.

- **Move snow only as far as you have to.** Most of the areas you'll need to clear—driveways, porches, sidewalks, patios—are generally shaped like a rectangle. Imagine the center of your current rectangle, and shovel snow from that middle point to its nearest edge.

- **Clear cars first.** After clearing the snow from the cars, shovel the areas around them.

- **Foreground first, background last.** Think back to your rectangle: First clear a strip along its perimeter and then push the snow from the center to the cleared area, where you can lift and toss the snow out of your cleared area.

- **Don't let yourself get dehydrated.** Bring water out with you, and be sure to drink it.

- **Take frequent breaks,** so your muscles aren't continually engaged in the strenuous activity. This will also help you remember to keep hydrated.

- **Do a thorough job, but don't get obsessive.** As you clear an area, you can sprinkle it with de-icer, and let the sun finish some of the job for you. When you remove snow and expose the ground, the surface is no longer as reflective, which helps the surrounding snow melt faster.

- **Dress appropriately.** It might be freezing as you first walk out the door, but after twenty minutes you'll have warmed up and possibly will be drenched in sweat. Dress in removable layers.

- **Enlist help.** Making it a team effort will make it more enjoyable as well as make it go faster.

- **Scatter de-icer in a thin but uniform layer.** Don't go overboard.
- **Be proactive.** If you're expecting a lot of snow, don't wait for all of it to come down before you start shoveling. Several light passes can be significantly easier than one mammoth job.
- **Keep your shovel in good shape.** If the edge is metal, use a hammer to flatten it if it gets bent out of shape. If it's plastic, use a utility knife to clean off the burrs that develop; they will blunt the shovel. If the shovel gets wobbly where it meets the handle, take a large hex-head sheet-metal screw and drive it through the shovel's collar (the part of the shovel that encircles the handle) and into the handle.
- **When you're finished, stretch again.** Use ice or ibuprofen for sore muscles, and continue to hydrate.

You also want to make sure that the way you're shoveling is the best for your body. To make sure you don't hurt yourself, remain aware of the proper body mechanics:

- Push the snow as much as you can, rather than lifting it. If you must lift at some point, do so with your legs and not your back.
- When rising upright from a squat position, keep your back straight.
- Try to use your shoulder muscles as much as possible.
- Keep the shovel as close to your upper body as possible.
- When lifting, keep one hand low on the handle toward the shovel blade for better leverage.
- When you toss the snow off your shovel, don't twist the upper half of your body.

Shoveling snow will never really be all that much fun, but at least now you know you'll do it perfectly!

Snow Hazard

A 2011 study in the *American Journal of Emergency Medicine* found that there are an average of 11,500 injuries related to snow shoveling in the United States each year, and that number only includes those that are treated in the emergency room. In the time period studied, heart attacks accounted for 7 percent of the injuries. Fifteen percent of these injuries were incurred by people under the age of eighteen, 20 percent from slipping and/or falling, and more than half from "acute musculoskeletal exertion."

WAY TO WASH YOUR HAIR

*W*e ask people how to do things every day. *How did you get your screensaver to do that? How do I get back to the highway? How did you get your golden retriever to stop barking at school buses?* But when was the last time you fumbled through the basic steps of washing your hair and afterward thought you should really ask someone if there is a way you could be doing this better?

In case you *were* wondering, you'll be happy to know that the researchers at Dove believe they have figured out the perfect way for you to wash your hair, and it only took six months and 500 volunteers to do so. The method is fairly specific:

- Temperature matters: For your shower, only use water at a temperature of 98°F.
- Measure the amount: For short hair use no more than 0.20 ounce of shampoo, for medium-length hair 0.27 ounce, and for long hair 0.34 ounce.
- Lather, rinse, repeat: Plan on lathering for a full twenty-eight seconds with twenty rub motions. Rinsing should take twenty-two seconds, and to make sure your hair is fully rinsed from root to end, repeat the rinse once.

- Conditioning is important: Research warns that conditioner is mandatory, and for short, medium, and long hair, you should use 0.07 ounce, 0.14 ounce, and 0.20 ounce of conditioner, respectively. Application of conditioner should be done with a wide-toothed comb and, before being rinsed with 98°F water, should be left in for fifty-seven seconds.
- Towel dry: The finishing touch is to pat your hair with a towel—not aggressively scrub it—and then rather than using a blow dryer, let your hair air-dry.

Celebrity stylist Charles Baker Strahan also recommends that you brush your hair *before* you shower, as wet hair is more fragile.

WEATHER

*I*n Minnesota in December, residents may think that perfect weather is 90°F and sunny. In Arizona in August, residents may be thinking something different. But when all is said and done, perfect weather is a temperature of 72°F–73°F, according to various studies and polls, most notably 2007's *Climate Preferences for Tourism* by D. Scott, S. Gössling, and C.R. de Freitas. The majority of people surveyed enjoyed a light breeze (0.6 to 5.6 miles per hour), no rain, and a partial cloud covering on a quarter of the sky. Not that they're specific or anything.

The importance of perfect weather in our lives is still debatable. While studies from the 1970s found a low mood associated with poor weather, more recent studies out of Germany show that weather actually has little effect on the mood of the general population. Ani Kalajian, a Fordham University psychology professor, says that may be due to the fact that "feelings are transient; we can change them, transform them into positive."

Despite our ever-changing moods, studies found climate is a top consideration for people when evaluating cities. Cities with sunny days and few rainy ones include:

- Los Angeles, California
- Phoenix, Arizona

- Albuquerque, New Mexico
- Santa Fe, New Mexico

In addition, Sedona, Arizona; San Diego, California; and Orlando, Florida, have the desired average temperatures of 72°F, although Orlando has a robust rainy season June to September.

Several cities also have perfect weather occasionally, just not all year round. London, England, fits the description of perfect in June, July, and August. Toronto, Canada, finds perfection in June, August, and September. And everyone loves New York City in May, June, and September.

Hawaii has such consistently "perfect weather" that some of its residents actually find it boring and too perfect. Hawaii was even described as "perfect weather, year-round" in a 2010 issue of *National Geographic*. The article, written by Katie Arnold, defined perfection as "mostly sunny, 75 degrees, give or take," and adds, "The Aloha State promises epic adventure, every time." So fire up the Tiki torches, don a lei, and pick an island.

WORST WEATHER CITIES

In 2011, *AOL News* declared Fargo, North Dakota, to be "America's Toughest Weather City" thanks to its "infamous blizzards, extreme cold, and spring floods." *Forbes* rated Cleveland, Ohio, as "America's Worst Winter Weather City," due to its average of 60 inches of snow every winter, and an average *annual* temp of only 50°F. Boston, Massachusetts, came in a close number two, due to its frequent nor'easters.

Afterword

*C*ongratulations! Never again will you serve your red wines too warm, fall for a fake smile, or skip the chicken soup when you have the sniffles. You are now significantly closer to perfection than you were before reading this book. Go ahead and digitally edit your face over DaVinci's Vitruvian Man. And then, maybe touch up the photo a little more. After all, the quest for perfection is neverending. Striving for improvement of ourselves and our world is part of the human condition, and the drive for improvement is in and of itself "perfect," as it causes positive growth for humanity. Whether it was a chef with a sandwich, or a scientist pioneering the boundaries of physics as we know them, each effort toward perfection brings discovery and improvement not just to the person searching, but those with whom they can share the information. So congratulations on your quest and happy hunting!

Index

ABOUT THE AUTHOR

TOM MOYNIHAN always strives for perfection and
has done so in a number of different professions.
While he's always looking to perfect perfection, he
enjoyed defining it in this book.

 **DAILY BENDER**

Want Some More?

Hit up our humor blog, The Daily Bender, to get your fill of all things funny—be it subversive, odd, offbeat, or just plain mean. The Bender editors are there to get you through the day and on your way to happy hour. Whether we're linking to the latest video that made us laugh or calling out (or bullshit on) whatever's happening, we've got what you need for a good laugh.

If you like our book, you'll love our blog. (And if you hated it, "man up" and tell us why.) Visit The Daily Bender for a shot of humor that'll serve you until the bartender can.

Sign up for our newsletter at
www.adamsmedia.com/blog/humor
and download our Top Ten Maxims No Man Should Live Without.